Don't Lie on Your Back
for a Guy
Who Doesn't Have Yours

America's Favorite Relationship Expert
Talks Tough to Young Women

by

DR. GILDA
CARLE

ACKNOWLEDGMENTS

Thank you to all who have so generously contributed your true stories to help others who are reading this book. Without your giving, there would be less healthful living!
--Dr. Gilda

Gilda-Gram®
SHOW guys
how you want to be treated,
by treating YOURSELF well!

TABLE OF CONTENTS

INTRODUCTION

Who's Got Your Back?   i

Part I
WHAT EVERY GIRL *WANTS*

Want #1: Loyal Girlfriends   2

Want #2: A Cool Boyfriend   38

Part II
WHAT EVERY GIRL *NEEDS*

Need #1: Be an *It Girl*   57

Need #2: Know How Guys Think   98

Need #3: Pursue Your Happy Places   164

Need #4: Accept Only "Got-Your-Back" 197
Love

CONCLUSION

You're In Charge!   211

INTRODUCTION
Who's Got Your Back?

The expression, "I've got your back" means "I'm looking out for you" and "I've got you covered, in case anyone badmouths you." The meaning of this expression is the same as "I've got your 6," which comes from the military. The "6" reflects the hour on a clock, with 12 o'clock in front of you, and 6 o'clock behind you. Have the guys you liked had your 6??

In November 2015, Charlie Sheen announced he had tested positive for HIV four years earlier. HIV is the virus that causes AIDS. Sheen's disclosure came years after he had bragged about all the drugs he had taken, and the 5,000 women he had bedded. He also shockingly admitted he had sex without a condom after his diagnosis. Then, it was reported that he was caught on video smoking crack and performing oral sex on another man in 2011, the same year he was diagnosed with HIV.

Question to you, my reader: Did Charlie Sheen have the backs of the women he might have infected with this deadly virus?

i

As soon as she found out that Charlie Sheen had HIV, Jenny McCarthy blasted him. She had played his love interest several times on "Two and a Half Men," from 2007 to 2011. She revealed she had to sign on-set releases about her having herpes cold sores, which could be contagious—but not deadly. So how was it okay, she wondered, for Sheen not to disclose his infection with HIV? Many other women had also played his love interest on the TV show.

Jenny McCarthy continued that before she married Donnie Wahlberg, when she was single and wanted to have sex with a guy, she insisted that he get an HIV test. She said, "There is nothing I want to do dumb enough to get any type of disease. I have to live forever for my (autistic) kid. So I wouldn't sleep with anyone until I got the right paperwork."

McCarthy called what Sheen had concealed as "not fair and scary." Other women with whom he had sex called it worse than that.

Charlie Sheen was reckless. And his sex partners were so numerous, who knows what the ramifications will eventually be? Was the thrill of having sex with a famous actor more important to these women than protecting themselves from a deadly disease? Apparently, it was—and it's too bad, because Sheen surely didn't have these women's best interests—or their backs—when he bedded them. Even after the news of Sheen's HIV status broke, he told a tabloid, "I should have been more responsible, and more concerned for myself [before he contracted the disease]." Note his concern for himself only!

When young women seek a boyfriend, they usually look for someone cute and popular—perhaps similar to a younger version of Charlie Sheen. And young women try hard to land that guy to like them. If he comes around, they're very happy. But they never consider whether he would extend himself for them.

Does the guy of your dreams inconvenience himself to make you happy? Does he defend you from mean people? Has he got your 6? Guys who "have your back," or guys who "have your 6," are guys who really and truly CARE. When a guy doesn't protect and defend his girlfriend, that girl becomes deeply hurt. Until now, did you even consider the necessity for a guy to cover your 6?

Some celebrities have. Kim Kardashian, Britney Spears, Heidi Klum, Kate Gosselin, Amy Winehouse, and Scarlett Johansson were romantically linked to their bodyguards. These guys won the stars' trust by spending much time with them to provide their safety. It's also the reason the 1992 movie, The Bodyguard, with Whitney Houston and Kevin Costner was such a hit. Even if a woman doesn't voice this, every single one of us wants to know our guy will protect us from possible harm.

The only problem is that younger women rarely think of this trait because they're so lost in a guy's hotness and popularity. Sadly, it's only after girls get hurt and have a few years behind them that they realize the value of a guy having their back!

It took me until I was in my 30s to recognize this vital lesson. I was in an exclusive relationship for 2 years with a guy who everyone called "the most eligible bachelor in New York." He was handsome, rich, athletic, fit, popular, and available. I didn't much seem to consider that he was also cheap, egocentric, and selfish. (Today, my Gilda-Gram® warns, "Cheap with money, cheap with love." If a guy is cheap, of course, he's also egocentric and selfish. But I was naïve back then and didn't know better.)

He and I were attending an elegant Hamptons summer party when I walked onto the outdoor patio, but missed the step down. Immediately, my ankle swelled. Where was my guy? Oh, as always, he was sweet-talking a group of adoring females, which he forever defended as "good for his business."

I called out to him, but he didn't hear. Finally, in terrible pain, I limped over to where he was holding court with the adoring women, and told him I twisted my ballooning ankle. I limped to a chair as Mr. Ego followed. I had to *tell* him to please get me some ice. He shuffled to the kitchen, fetched some loose ice cubes, wrapped them in a paper towel that quickly became wet and torn, haphazardly delivered the cold wad to my hand (not my ankle), and left me to return to his admiring crowd. I felt like a blob of chopped liver. "What am I doing here?," I wondered.

After two years of my performing all the emotional lifting for this clueless lothario, as I writhed in pain, all Dude could muster were a few loose ice cubes carelessly thrown into my palm!

This guy had no idea how to give or how to inconvenience himself for someone he said he "loved." My ankle survived, but from that day on, my romance with him was history.

As he was exiting my life, he thought he was being generous when he announced he had never physically cheated on me. *Duh!* From this misguided relationship, I saw that cheating is more than slipping Flap A into Slot B. What really mattered is that Dude never had my back. And he was so enmeshed in himself, he never could.

As my Gilda-Gram® advises, "When something happens TO you, it really happens FOR you." I gratefully thanked my ankle injury for all the light it had cast. This guy's looks, popularity, and charm were secondary to having a man who was devoted to *me and me alone.*

A few years later, I ran into someone who told me the lothario had gotten married. I pitied his unknowing bride. Then a year after that, someone else revealed the big scandal in that very ritzy crowd that Dude was openly cheating on his wife. I was not surprised, but I was also glad I had not been the one to marry him. How I had dodged that bullet!

Tech savvy young women spend more time online than they do building relationship skills offline. As you will see from the emails I receive, many girls are not practiced when it comes to real life interactions with girlfriends and boyfriends. As a result, too many are taken advantage of by users and losers.

After I wrote my best seller, *Don't Bet on the Prince! How to Have the Man You Want by Betting on Yourself,* I received lots of sorrowful emails from adult women and teen girls throughout the world. Quickly, I concluded that all women's issues are similar.

Young and old, everyone wanted to know how to find Mr. Right and keep Mr. Right; how to make friends into boyfriends, and how to make boyfriends into friends; how not to get dumped, and what to do if that happened; and how to cope with lying, cheating, and love triangles.

At once, I saw that the unresolved issues girls had with their boyfriends grew into the same issues that perplexed older women in relationships with men.

Every time a girl seeks my advice about a guy who's hurt her, I ask, "Did you see the red flags?" "Did you split from your guy the first time he showed you disrespect?" "Or did you stick around, hoping he'd change—or worse, that you'd be able to change him?"

Most girls have never been taught to be selective. They never learned that a) they have choices, b) they deserve to find guys who have their backs, and c) if a guy disses them, it's not their job to reform him. If this is how he is, this is how he'll stay—unless HE chooses to change.

Some years ago, a study of 15,000 girls from 13 to 20, found that the top reason girls have sex is because of curiosity, not love. While more than 75 percent of the girls said it was important to be in love with a guy before having sex with him, only 58 percent said they were. Forty-five percent thought the guy loved them, 20 percent felt pressured, and almost half of those who became sexually active, most at age 15, agreed they had been too young. Most non-virgin teen girls say they're sorry they didn't wait.

"Don't Lie on Your Back for a Guy Who Doesn't Have Yours" shows young women how to protect themselves from the not-so-good guys, and instead find guys that are cool. By protecting themselves, I don't mean only using condoms and other birth control—although that's a must if they're having sex. But also, girls must learn to protect themselves emotionally, so they are able to limit the hurts they suffer from a guy who didn't have their 6.

Many young women are obsessed with having a boyfriend. This book will teach you how to calm down long enough to attract someone who won't give you grief and who is worthy of you.

Sadly, most girls don't realize how much power they have. Several studies prove that girls are emotionally sturdier than boys, and their healthy development is most harmed when they are restricted or confined. Yet many girls long to confine themselves to one steady boyfriend, believing he will be the answer to all their prayers.

This book explains why that's a bad idea. You'll learn how to develop your own skills and pursue your education, so you'll find fulfilling relationships *when you're ready*. Young women who apply their power avoid becoming victims of pain. They know how to stay away from the wrong guys. They know love doesn't have to hurt.

Gilda-Gram®
We attract not who we want,
but WHO WE ARE.

Celebrate your uniqueness. In this book, you'll recognize you are the *real* Number One in every relationship you have, no matter how hot you think a guy may be! And your place as Number One must never, never, never change.

From all the experience I've had with young women, I know you want to hear this information straight. A lot of females sit on their feelings and put up with poor treatment. Yet they'd never accept abuse from one of their girlfriends.

But with guys, girls don't want to rock the boat,

to seem like they're too much trouble. Adult women often do the same dumb thing. Instead of calling a guy out on his bad behavior as soon as it begins, they suffer in silence, and accept things as they are. Oh, they'll complain to their girlfriends, but they won't say a word to the guy! When they've finally become really miserable, still they won't confront the guy. Instead, they contact me.

Look at these two emails. One is from a grown woman and the other is from a teen girl. Notice how similar they are.

Dear Dr. Gilda,
I'm a 52-year-old woman who's in love with Tom, who's 62. We have a "commitment" issue, which, in his mind, means he doesn't sleep with anyone but me. But he escorts female "friends" to various social events and flirts with women constantly, right in front of my eyes.

I'm furious he doesn't take our relationship seriously. I feel disrespected and humiliated. Although I've told Tom how I feel, he has not changed his behavior. What should I do?
Carol

Dear Dr. Gilda,
I'm 14 and I've been dating Jon for two months. After a few weeks of knowing each other, I was starting to fall for him more than any other boy. Last week, we got into a big fight about his flirting with other girls and

asking them to have sex with him.

When I told him I was angry, he said, "Oh, honey, you know I love you, and when I say that stuff I'm not serious." So I believed him. Finally, one day at school, he was being really mean to me, not waiting for me where we usually meet, ditching me to walk off with my best friend, and telling me on the phone how hot she is. I've been crying myself to sleep for a week. What should I do?
Janice

There is almost 40 years' difference between the ages of these two females. Yet both are miserable because a guy made them think they had an exclusive relationship. Then they discovered he had a different meaning for "exclusive" than they did.

What is the problem here? Why are young women suffering the same disappointment with their boyfriends that grown women are?

Learn to be selective about who you fall for while you're young, and you'll have the skills you need to avoid the painful separations and divorces that sadly emerge too often when you're older. In this book, you'll learn to take care of Number One. Girlfriend, Number One is and always should be YOU!

Females are usually not good at their own caretaking because they've been taught to be the caretakers of others, not only *first*, but often *instead of* themselves. But women who give to others before or instead of giving to themselves become stressed, burned out, and angry when they realize no one's there for them. You've got only one person to nurture above all else, and that is YOU.

<u>Gilda-Gram®</u>
If you don't protect yourself,
who will?

Gilda-Grams®, like the ones above, are feel-good statements you can repeat and remember when you need a boost. Say them or write them, and see how they quickly improve your mood.

In the next chapters, you will learn what girls *want* and what girls *need*. What people *want* is what they'd *like to have*. What they *need* is what they *have to have* to live a happy life.

Young women tell me the two things you *want* most in your social life are loyal girlfriends and a cool boyfriend. But to get the *right* girlfriends and boyfriends, you *need* to:

1. project with confidence that you're Number One

2. understand what makes guys tick

3. create your own happy places

4. nurture a guy's friendship before seeking his love

These are *your* personal needs, not those of the girlfriends and guys you hang with. Note that a strong YOU is necessary before pursuing a good guy.

<u>Gilda-Gram®</u>
We attract the types of people we ARE.

Follow the guidelines in this book to become the best you can be. That's how you'll attract the best, most considerate, and caring guy.
xoxo,
Dr. Gilda

PART I

WHAT EVERY GIRL *WANTS*

WANT #1

Loyal Girlfriends

Many years ago, a woman by the name of Linda Tripp taped the personal and private conversations of a supposedly good friend of hers, Monica Lewinsky. She then played back these private conversations for the whole world to hear. The reason people were so interested in this story was because Lewinsky was in an intimate relationship with Bill Clinton, President of the United States.

When Linda Tripp revealed Monica Lewinsky's private information, females around the world were appalled that a so-called "friend" would do such an evil thing. Every female alive knows what a sacred bond it is to confide in a special friend. Most of us have had the painful experience of trusting someone with a secret because we thought that someone was a friend. When our private information is blabbed about behind our back, we're embarrassed—and furious.

Interestingly, when a female bonobo ape gets unwanted sexual attention from one of the male apes, she sounds a distress call, and her female buddies come

running to her rescue. THEY WATCH HER BACK!
The strong bonds they maintain with other females
defend them against troublemaking males.

The same kind of bonding usually exists with
loyal girlfriends. Yet sometimes there is interference,
and what was once a great friendship can fall apart. Gail
and her friends lived in a nice community in Maryland.
One of their good guy friends, Greg, moved to South
Carolina because his father had been transferred with his
job. Since they were all so close, whenever Greg had a
school break, he returned to his old neighborhood to
visit. Usually, he stayed at his best friend Cindy's
house.

One Friday night, Cindy took Greg to a party.
While he was there, he hooked up with Rosemarie.
When he returned to Cindy's house, he noticed that she
was decidedly cool. He asked her what was wrong, but
she blankly said, "Nothing."

The next day was Saturday, and there was no
school. Cindy called Rosemarie to confess she really
liked Greg, but she had never told him. She told
Rosemarie that she was angry at her for hooking up with
him under her nose. Rosemarie became angry, telling
Cindy that if she had known she liked Greg, she would
have deemed him "off limits."

When Monday came, two other girls at the party,
Andrea and Holly, were deep in conversation over Greg.
Andrea told Holly that Greg was coming from South

Carolina to visit her during the coming weekend. Rosemarie got wind of this, and became furious, not with Andrea for snatching the guy she laid claim to, but with Holly!

Getting angry at Holly instead of Andrea made sense to Rosemarie, because she was afraid of getting into a dispute with Andrea, the school bigmouth. So Rosemarie thought it was safer to lodge her anger against Holly. When Holly discovered Rosemarie's anger toward her, she in turn got angry at Rosemarie for being angry at her. Suddenly, everyone was fighting over one guy!

Rosemarie and Holly were good friends. They saw that things had gotten out of control. They decided to take a breath and reconsider. Each admitted that since Andrea is such a gossip, neither of them wanted to get in her face. Each agreed that Andrea could be a "big bitch," and they didn't want her to turn other girls against them.

They decided to do more digging. They found that Andrea had told them a lie. Greg had no intention of coming to Maryland to see her. Besides, everyone knew that when he visited his old community, it was Cindy he always stayed with--but now, since Cindy had a secret crush on Greg who didn't return her feelings, it was doubtful she would invite him again.

After everything was over, both girls were relieved they had not fallen into the trap of allowing another girl, and a liar as well, to bring down their friendship. These girls were smart enough to end their dispute immediately.

While guys often brag about their success to each other, girls cherish their friendships above all else. They'd like to believe their friends will protect their secrets and reputations.

Female friends offer a special brand of emotional connection that guys never experience with their buddies. For girls, friends are the sounding boards for what's right or wrong, good or bad, moral or immoral. Based on their friends' responses, they decide who they are and who they are going to become. When an intruder like Andrea tries to come between friends, smart girls band together.

Most girls feel better after discussing their issues with their good friends. Even before a girl notices that guys are on the planet, she invests her time and emotions in her friends. Thirteen-year-old Laurie observed that before high school, her focus had been on family, friends, and school--in that order. But once she got to high school, her focus changed to friends as her first priority, school as second, and family as last. Yes, friends are very important as girls grow.

When a girl becomes boy-obsessed, it's her friends who enjoy every detail of each crush. During a romance, a girl's friends are there to help her figure out what the guy's actions *really* mean. (Unless the girl is so involved with her guy that she drops her friends altogether—which too many girls stupidly do--until they learn that boys can never replace the friendships girlfriends provide.)

When a girl and her guy end their romance, it's her friends who make her feel better, and shield her from the pain the breakup caused. When she's between guys, her friends go out with her to search for new ones. But when a friend suddenly backstabs her, it's more upsetting than if it had been a guy who had done it.

Since friendships help you discriminate between good and evil, they provide important links to reality. Most importantly, the finding and keeping of girlfriends is good training *before* hooking up with a guy. The added bonus is that the way to deal with girlfriends follows the same game plan as the way to deal with guys.

All relationships--whether with girls or guys--draw from two parts of your personality: 1) your inner self and 2) your outer self. Your inner self is where you spend time alone, pursue favorite interests, and enjoy who you are as an individual. It is the place where you do your deepest thinking and have personal conversations with yourself that only you know about.

Your outer self is where you enjoy support and encouragement from other people, including your friends. Friends are outside your private world, and they are meant to build on the inner self you've already established.

<u>Gilda-Gram®</u>
**Friendships *enhance*
your already-strong inner self.**

If your friends gossip about you behind your
back, put you down, criticize you, and make you feel
bad, they are not enhancing your inner self. To enhance
who you already are, friends should build you up,
encourage you to pursue your dreams, and give you a
general feeling of joy when they're around you. Overall,
they should be able to do more for you when you're with
them than you can do for yourself when you're alone.

Even if you've had a friend for a long time with
whom you have closely bonded, other people, events,
and things can often get in the way. For example, a new
girl moves into your class, and you find that you want to
spend more time with her than with your best friend. Or
your parents have you on early curfew, but your friend's
folks think it's okay for her to stay out 'til midnight. Or
your friend has hooked up with a new guy who she is
always with, and you feel like you're out in the cold.
These situations can cause rifts between you and a
friend, even after you've been together for many years.

Changing your friendships might not feel
comfortable, but it's a fact of life. Changing our likes,
our wants, and our tastes is part of the way we grow.
Consider this: When you are 22, do you want to still
think as you did when you were 12? Of course not!

Even though people keep changing and

developing, in order for a friendship to last, it must be nurtured by *both* friends. If two people want to get together, they must create time for each other, even through the distractions. If their schedules are packed, they need to arrange times in advance, so they can continue to enjoy the activities they always did.

Gilda-Gram®
To *have* a good friend,
***be* a good friend.**

Do you consider yourself a good friend? For each of the following situations, choose one response.

How Good A Friend Are You?

1. Marney is crushing on a new guy who just moved to her school. She and Beth have been best friends for six years, but now Marney is acting boy-crazy, following this guy around, bumping into him at his locker, and staring at him. Beth thinks Marney's making a fool of herself. She:

    _____a) levels with Marney about how foolish she looks, and recommends other ways of getting this guy's attention.

    _____b) goes along with and encourages Marney's silly behavior, because she doesn't want to lose their friendship.

    _____c) admits to herself that Marney is acting ridiculous, does not want any part of it,

and ends the friendship with a simple
"See ya."

2. Carolyn has just become interested in
basketball, a passion her best friend, Janette, doesn't
share. Carolyn begins to go to their school's basketball
games, hangs out with other basketball fans, and seems
to be drifting away from the friendship the two shared
for three years. Janette is hurt that Carolyn has almost
totally dropped her, and she tells Carolyn she's upset.
Carolyn:

_____a) admits she's been distracted by her new
passion. She apologizes to Janette, and
asks her to come to the next basketball
game, telling her she doesn't want to end
their friendship. When Janette declines to
go, Carolyn suggests doing something else
together.

_____b) tells Janette she'll forego attending the
next game so she can be with her.

_____c) says, "Tough! You and I have different
interests now, and I don't think we have
much in common any more." She
completely drops their friendship.

3. Millie is in the library studying for her next
final, when she overhears her best friend, Sara, giggling
to another girl that Millie is too immature and ugly to
attract a guy. Millie had considered Sara a best friend,
so she's shocked to hear her backstabbing. Millie:

_____a) walks over to Sara, looks her straight in the

eyes, and just stares, showing her she heard everything. She doesn't say a word.

_____b) rises from her desk and screams at Sara that she's a two-faced bitch who can't be trusted.

_____c) ignores the incident, deciding that Sara is so popular, it pays to continue the friendship despite her two-faced actions.

4. Maureen just started smoking cigarettes and pot. Now she's pressuring her best friend, Kris, to do the same. Kris is on the swimming team, and knows how detrimental smoking is to her athletic performance. Yet she's torn, because Maureen has been a great friend who she doesn't want to lose. Kris:

_____a) levels with Maureen and tells her, "Sorry, smoking is just not for me."

_____b) lies that her uncle had lung cancer, and she made a promise to her mother never to put smoke into her lungs.

_____c) gives in, just to continue to be in Maureen's popular crowd.

5. A new girl just moved next door to Meri. It hasn't taken her long to get tight with the "fast" crowd, which Meri's mom has observed. Meri's mother has forbidden Meri to get friendly with this girl. The new girl is assigned to the seat next to Meri in math class. When they bump into each other outside their homes,

the girl asks Meri to leave her test paper uncovered tomorrow during their final exam, so she can copy her answers. Meri:

_____a) tells her mom, and explores the best way to handle this dilemma. The next day, she tells the new girl she doesn't want to get in trouble for cheating.

_____b) says okay, so she won't make an enemy of this popular girl or her friends.

_____c) stays home from school on the day of the test.

ScoreCard

Take 20 points for each (a); 10 points for each (b); 5 points for each (c).

75-100: Your friends can count on your loyalty. Keep doing what you have been.

50-75: Be stronger in sticking to your values, instead of being swayed by your friends, regardless of what they say.

25-50: You need to be honest about your feelings. Your beliefs are your own brand of who you are.

The 5 Rules of Friendship

When any relationship breaks up, we get hurt.

When young women ask for my advice about their friendship issues, I share these 5 Rules of Friendship:

1. Don't let guys come between you.

2. Schedule specific time for your friends.

3. If a friend backstabs you, confront her in a way she will hear.

4. If a friend pressures you to do things you're not comfortable with, stand your ground.

5. Share your friendship issues with your parents.

<u>Rule #1</u>
Don't Let Guys
Come between You and Your Friends

Dear Dr. Gilda,

I have a major problem. My two best friends and I are in the biggest fight of our lives! Blair and I have been best friends since second grade. We've been through everything from crushes to thoughts of suicide. Keegan and I met last year. I fell in love with him, but we stayed just friends. Last month, Keegan and I had an extra credit project, so he came to my house. Next thing I knew, we were making out.

I told two people, Blair and one other girl (it totally slipped out). Somehow, Keegan's best boy bud found out, and was teasing him. Keegan totally blew up at me (which I totally understand and I've already apologized). To get back at me, he started flirting with Blair, who actually flirted back!!

I know Blair's liked him forever, but I was the one who liked him first, and I was also the one who introduced them. I hate her now, and won't talk to her. She didn't even apologize for making a jackass of herself. I still want Keegan for a friend. What do I do??
Sad But Also Mad

Dear Sad But Also Mad,

This *is* a major problem, because you trusted both these people, and now they've turned on you. It makes you wonder whom you *can* trust, especially in the future. Girls should follow my rule of never letting a guy come between them.

What's up with Blair that she's so desperate for a guy? Or does she admire you so much that she wants what you have--even if it means your boyfriend? For friends who have been together since second grade, she sure has shown a lapse of judgment. And no one can blame you for feeling you hate her now. But hating anyone wastes your energy.

Would you feel comfortable having a heart-to-heart with her, telling her how you feel? Maybe she'll hear how hurt you are, and see the error of her ways. But if she doesn't, you're better off without her. Friends need to be trustworthy.

As for Keegan, understand how embarrassed he was because of your wagging, bragging tongue. Guys don't like to be embarrassed in front of their friends, especially when it comes to mushy romance. You can continue to apologize to him for your lapse of judgment, and see if he will forgive you. Truthfully, he may be too uncomfortable to talk to you for some time.

Most importantly, I hope you've learned your lesson about talking about your personal business.
Dr. Gilda

Even after a romance has ended, wanting to go out with a best friend's ex could be tricky.

Dear Dr. Gilda,

My best friend told me she likes my ex-boyfriend, and wouldn't mind going out with him. He dumped me 6 months ago, and I'm still not over him. I would definitely have a problem with this. Am I being selfish?

NJ

Dear NJ,

If this girl were a casual acquaintance who didn't know your feelings for this guy, I'd say you can't fault her. But this is your *best friend.* She's the selfish one! I have this rule: Best friends can share crises, clothes, and comments. But they should not share boyfriends.

Maybe if you were completely over him, you'd feel differently. But you're not--and she knows it--so she ought to be more sensitive to your feelings. Tell her that. Also share how disappointed in her you are.

Of course, she'll do whatever she wants to do anyway. But after you confront her, her actions will tell you whether you want to keep her friendship.

Dr. Gilda

When girls let guys get between them, there are many hurt feelings. Since friends have a lot in common, it's not unusual for two friends to like the same guy. But usually, the one who liked him first is the one who lays claim, while the other respects her friend's choice.

15

Most girls follow this "unwritten" agreement, which no one ever discusses. But there are often lots of problems when one girl decides it's open season on another girl's man. Note how the following twosome worked it out.

Throughout her years in school, Ellen, now 14, had had about ten different boyfriends, so she was aware that boys would come and go in her life. During Christmas break, a group of Ellen's girlfriends decided to go skating at their town's ice skating rink. Ellen's best friend, Katrina, couldn't go because of a bad cold. Ellen went anyway with five other girls.

As she skated around the rink, falling and flopping with her giddy girlfriends, one of the guys from school came up to her. As she was slipping on the ice for the tenth time, Jeff always came to her rescue. She and Jeff began to skate around the rink for an hour, laughing and joking.

As she was leaving, Ellen realized she liked Jeff. However, she also recognized this presented a dilemma, because Katrina was already going out with him. She didn't share this information with her best friend, even though they discussed *everything*.

Instead, Ellen held her feelings in, and felt guilty for having them. She remembered when another boy had tried to come between them, and almost ruined their friendship. Now she was determined to stick to the rule that she and Katrina created after that event: "Chicks before Dicks."

Being a trustworthy friend, Ellen honored their agreement. She concluded, "Jeff is out of the picture. These days I like Sean."

Not everyone chooses to solve her love issues so maturely. Morgan and her best friend seem to enjoy exchanging guys, and for them, it's all right.

Dear Dr. Gilda,
I hope you can help me. I have a crush on this guy, but he's my best friend's ex, and he still loves her. He's not very cute, but he's really nice. My best friend likes him too, but she's already got a DORKY, FREAKISH, JERKY, UGLY, NASTY, OBNOXIOUS, BONEHEAD of a boyfriend. He's my ex...unfortunately.

I really like my best friend's ex a lot. He's sending me mixed signals. I don't know what to do. Please help me.
Morgan

Dear Morgan,
You are crushing on someone who still loves someone else. Are there only two guys in your town? Why are you willing to take your friend's cast-offs?

You're setting yourself up for heartache, since you already know he's still devoted to your friend. Are you secretly trying to get back at her for running off with your ex? When you believe you deserve more than

crumbs, you'll go for someone who's available.
Dr. Gilda

Each case is different, and every girl has a different feeling about whether it's okay for her friends to date her ex. For some it doesn't matter, but for others, the wounds cut deep. Know in advance how your friends feel about this issue.

Each girl deserves to be cherished for the special person she is. She can be cherished by her girlfriends, as well as by a guy. But one relationship should not interfere with another.

Rule #2
Schedule Specific Time
for Your Friends

Since everyone is busy, it's easy to find yourself drifting away from friends you once spent a lot of time with. As we grow, we develop new interests, which lead to new friendships. This can be hurtful for the friends we leave behind.

Dear Dr. Gilda,
Alicia and I started hanging out together at the beginning of the year. Then this girl she knew from a few years ago started hanging out with her. This new person began dragging her everywhere, and she won't hang out with me anymore. I want to tell Alicia how I feel, but I can never get her alone. I also have no one else to hang with. Will Alicia ever realize I want to hang with her, and if not, how do I tell her?
Louise

Dear Louise,
Obviously you're hurting because Alicia left you for someone else. Being replaced doesn't make anyone feel good. But what makes your predicament especially painful is that Alicia seems to be your only friend. That is a dangerous situation because, as you have seen, if something happens to that one friendship, you are left

empty by having no one at all.

The way to protect yourself from feeling alone is to have one or two *great* friends, but also to cultivate other friends, as well. These others may not be as close to you as your best friends, but you can still enjoy being with them.

Instead of spending your energy worrying about whether Alicia will or won't realize you want to still hang with her, invest your time in finding more friends. Get into the things you love to do, and meet people who enjoy the same things.
Dr. Gilda

Friends do grow apart, because they no longer share the same interests. Accept that, and move on gracefully. While you are enjoying your own favorite activities, you'll meet friends who mirror your tastes.

Rule #3
If a Friend Backstabs You,
Confront Her
in a Way She'll Hear

Nobody deserves a friend who can't be trusted. Friends are supposed to support you, and cover your back. Sometimes a friend we've trusted becomes jealous or nasty or whatever--and we become not only disappointed, but also angry that this person turned on us. Then the question is, "Should I confront the friend who backstabbed me? And if so, how?"

To confront anyone who has hurt you, question whether you'll be dealing with this person again. If she's someone you'll never see again, or at least will see rarely, forget her and move on.

But if she's someone you will continue to run into, if she still hangs with your best buds, or if you have some classes in common, you might want to clear the air by letting her know you heard her negative comments about you. However, if you become too accusatory, she'll only come back with, "No, I didn't," or "You don't know what you're talking about." Instead, it's best to be direct and honest in your confrontation.

These same principles work in love. Psychologist John Gottman has found that the best relationships are those in which two people confront and repair their incidents quickly.

Successful Confrontation

Before you choose to tell someone off, decide what you want to accomplish. If you scream, yell, and curse at her, all she'll hear is your anger. She may come back at you with similar screaming, yelling, and cursing. A catfight is not what you need. Instead, be honestly upfront with her in a way she will hear.

    a.   For a successful confrontation, follow these 3 Steps:

        1)   "When you said (or did)...,

        2)   I felt..."

        3)   Stop.

The last Step, Stop, is a separate Step because Steps 1 and 2 are so powerful. The person you're confronting will probably listen to the way in which her actions affected the way you *felt*.

No normal person wants to be the one accused of hurting someone. Because your listener is suddenly hearing you, maybe even for the first time, you might be tempted to tell her about *all* the times you felt awful as a result of her behavior. Instead, follow the Stop sign, and put a lid on it. Less is more.

After your confrontation, your so-called "friend" might feel bad or embarrassed. She may try to offer some lame excuse, which will probably be some lie like, "I never did that," or "Tom didn't really understand what I was saying when he said I said that." It doesn't matter what this chick's comeback is. What does matter is that you got your grief *off your own chest*. If your friend is embarrassed, too bad!

Confrontation is not the most comfortable thing in the world. But this technique is more *for you* than it is for your friend, because when you let her know you're on to her, you take total control. Confrontation therefore has two main benefits:

1) It lets your friend know you won't allow anyone to *act* like a friend, but turn on you when you're not looking.

2) It teaches you how to stick up for yourself so no one will get away with trashing you.
These are important lessons!

What you decide to do after you've heard your friend's excuses is up to you. You might want to give her a second chance (and if she wants to keep you as a friend, she'll now be on her best behavior), or you might want to permanently ditch the two-faced foe.

It really doesn't matter what you decide, because now you're in control--and everyone around you will know it. Enjoy your new, bold power!

Now that you know to successfully confront someone, how would you handle this sticky situation?

Dear Dr. Gilda,
I visited my family in another state over Christmas vacation. When I came back, my best friend said she slept with my boyfriend while I was gone. He swears nothing happened. The other people at the party where this supposedly happened are saying nothing happened between them. What do I do about this? HELP!!
S.S.

Readers, before you hear my solution, think about how you would respond if this happened to you. It's her best friend who has said this, and she probably sees her every day. Here's what I told S.S.:

Dear S.S.,
What kind of "best" friend do you have? Why would she even say this to you--or do such a thing--if it even occurred? This so-called friend is obviously looking to hurt your feelings. If her tale is true, of course, you must dump her. But even if it's false and she's making it up, the question is WHY does she want to make you suffer?

Look for signs from your boyfriend to determine if his feelings for you have changed. Forget about what the other people at the party said, unless they were acting as his bodyguard during the night. A relationship is between you and your boyfriend, not between you, your boyfriend, and others. The basis of every relationship must be trust.

You surely are not getting respect from your girlfriend. But if you find you're also not getting what you deserve from your guy, move on.
Dr. Gilda

Nobody needs a two-timing best friend. The only question now is whether S.S. feels the need to confront her "friend." Will she be running into her again? How will she feel when she sees her? If S.S. feels the need to set the record straight and tell her how she feels, then confrontation is the way to go.

<u>Rule #4</u>
If You Feel Pressured to Do Something
You Don't Want to Do,
Stand Your Ground

Sometimes your good friends will drink, smoke, use drugs, or do slutty things. These behaviors may not sit well with you.

<u>Gilda-Gram®</u>
Life is about making choices.

According to one survey, teen pressures include getting good grades, getting into college, fitting in socially, and using drugs and alcohol. Saying "no" to any or all of these takes courage. It is ultimately *your choice*--not anyone else's--to decide what is right for you. But choosing is not only your right, it's your obligation to yourself.

<u>Gilda-Gram®</u>
It is YOU who will suffer
the consequences of your actions.

If you see a friend going down the wrong path, as a supportive friend, you may want to advise her about some of the consequences of her behavior, as these girls want to do with their friend. Sometimes that works, and sometimes that doesn't.

Dear Dr. Gilda,

We're 13 and our best friend is 12, and she is, well, put it this way, not a virgin!! She has had sex and does several other things that 12-year-olds should not be doing! Every time she goes out with someone, she tries to get him in bed.

All her friends are telling her she shouldn't be doing things like that at her age, but she says she loves these boys. We know she doesn't know what love is. What should we do?
Her concerned friends,
Sherry and Cassie

Dear Sherry and Cassie,

You girls are very kind to advise your promiscuous friend about the consequences of her behavior. Too bad she won't listen.

She may resent your butting into her life, and this could be the beginning of the parting of your ways. People are judged by their associations, and if your friend's behavior is slutty and she won't listen to your advice, you may not want to be judged as slutty, too. This is up to you.

The best you can do is make your pitch to your friend, hear her reactions, and then decide if it's worth the consequences for you to remain in her social circle.
Dr. Gilda

Girls need to develop a strong inner self, so they will feel comfortable making the right choices. The question about values is always yours alone to decide. With a strong inner self, you will foresee consequences of bad behavior before you're perhaps even tempted.

But there is a warning. Sometimes, sticking to your values can be lonely. New research from Harvard has found that there is definitive bias against girls and women who are leaders. And who doesn't like these females? Teen boys, teen girls, and even parents! Admit they might be intimidated by your strength. But that's their problem, not yours!

Gilda-Gram®
**Everyone is not always
going to love you.**

If you choose an unpopular view, some of your friends might badmouth you or try to pressure you into going along with them. When you've accepted that you can't be popular to everyone, you'll know your inner self is getting stronger.

Rule #5
Share Your Friendship Issues
with Your Parents

A USA Today Teen Panel of 25 members concluded that growing up usually means growing away from your parents. To become independent, teens want less parental togetherness, and more time to spend with friends. Consequently, parents feel cast aside. I don't often hear from a parent like this one, who actually appreciates the boyfriend her daughter has.

Dear Dr. Gilda,
My 16-year-old daughter is in love with a sweet, wonderful, caring, generous man of 21. They have a great relationship, built on communication, respect, and trust. Due to their ages, I realize the chances that they will eventually drift apart. My friends think I'm crazy to allow them to be together. It would be possible for me to send him away, but my daughter is so much happier and well adjusted with him, I see no reason to do that.

He refuses to have intercourse, not because of her age, but because he wants to wait until he marries. They do engage in other sexual activities, though. My question is this: Is it ever appropriate for a 16-year-old girl (she's not a virgin) and a 21-year-old man to be

romantically involved?
Sincerely,
Jean Jones

Dear Jean,

You seem to be one of the most level headed
parents I've heard from. When it comes to love,
anything is possible. Of course, at 16, your daughter
can't possibly know what she'll want when she's older.
And even a man of 21 is not mature enough to map out
his entire life's plan at this time. But since you
recognize they are good for each other, and since there's
no possibility of pregnancy or STD's, why can't this
romance run its course?

Your daughter has experienced other sexual
encounters, yet she's in no hurry to press her boyfriend
for sex now. I'd say you're doing the right thing in
supporting the romance's progression. You know where
she is, you know with whom, you trust them both, and
she'll either grow with him, or take what she needs to
learn from the experience, and move on.

Your support of her choices does her a great deal
of good. Unlike most girls her age, she won't get into
the usual rebelliousness with you for trying to constrict
her.

I wish there were more rational moms out there
like you. No wonder your daughter chose her man so
wisely!
Dr. Gilda

Unlike this mom, sometimes your parents won't
like your friends, and they will demand you to break off

ties with them. Since you probably won't agree with their values, you'll end up in conflict. Other times, a friend's parents may not like you for some reason. Then your friend will try to sway them to her way of thinking.

Dear Dr. Gilda,

I'm a 16-year-old girl with a huge problem. My best friend is Susan. Her parents hate me, and they won't let her be around me. I've talked to Susan about it, but she says she can't stand up to them about it. I don't know why they hate me. I'm a good person, and I know what I want in life.

A couple of years ago, Susan and I were best friends, but we got into a terrible argument that included both sets of parents screaming at each other, and Susan and I didn't speak for a year. But now we're in the same classes, and we've become best friends again. Could parents hold a grudge that long?
Juliet

Dear Juliet,

Parents don't want to see their kids get hurt. So to protect them, they set rules they believe will save their teens from pain. One of the rules that Susan's parents set was meant to protect their daughter from getting into the same terrible situation again with you as she had in the past.

Of course, both you girls believe you're older and wiser now that it's a year later, and that your parents should forget the past. Maybe yours have. But Susan's parents are still being protective of their daughter.

31

Susan should try to slowly re-introduce you to her parents as a new, mature friend. At the same time, she should level with her folks about some of the issues she is having in learning to trust you again.

If she is honest with them, and open about trying to mend the past, they may begin to see their daughter as capable of making wiser decisions than she had a year ago. But it will take time, so be patient.
Dr. Gilda

Okay, let's get real. No matter where your folks come from, no matter what their educational background or financial status, they have one objective in mind: to protect their child--YOU--from harm.

<u>Gilda-Gram®</u>
Parents never give impartial advice.

Parents always have this hidden agenda, so recognize where they're coming from. If you get upset with their decisions about your life, keep in mind they may be acting in two roles--one, as your overprotective parents, and two, as your unpaid guardian angel. Sure, the first role can be a real pain and their tastes might seem warped, but should you need the second one--and who doesn't need a guardian angel occasionally?--look at what you have as an added bonus.

Again, you have choices. You can reject the interference--as well as the benefits--from having concerned parents, or you can let your folks in on your life and your choices, so they can help you when you do need them. It's your decision.

Sure you want to be independent. You want to have your own life. You want to break away. As you have seen, making choices is a way of being a grownup. Grownups have to choose between potentially sticky possibilities.

Making a choice about this issue now is good training for your later years, when you'll need to choose between things far more important.

Girls who let their parents get to know their friends stand a better chance of their parents trusting their judgments. That translates to less hassle for you in the long run. When parents feel they know what's going on in their daughter's life, the more they'll trust that she's not trying to hide anything from them, and that she's safe. That mutual trust provides big payoffs. Sasha felt those payoffs after confiding in her mom.

On the day she moved into Sasha's neighborhood, a new girl, Krissy, came to the school dance. Sasha saw that Krissy wore a slutty outfit that immediately won her acceptance into the popular crowd. Just a week later, Krissy confided to Sasha that she and another popular friend had stolen $160 worth of clothes from a local store.

Sasha wanted to be in the popular crowd herself, but she knew Krissy's actions were wrong. She told her mom, and her mom said she didn't want her to be friends with Krissy. Sasha didn't know what to do, because she still wanted acceptance by this popular crowd. She didn't feel comfortable admitting that part to her mother. So she put off making her decision.

Then Krissy suddenly acted mean towards her. Now, without hesitation, Sasha said goodbye. Sasha admits she's glad she's not friends with Krissy anymore. She hears that she drinks, smokes, and gets into trouble with the police.

Sasha's also glad she told her mom, because it made her see the light, even if she was slow to follow her mother's advice. Parents can make surprisingly good allies when you need them.

How Loyal Are Your Friends?

Now that you've assessed whether you're a good friend yourself, you're in a better position to judge the reliability of your friends toward you. Just as it is with guys, when we first meet new girlfriends, they are on their best behavior. But if we let them in too soon, we may find they hurt us. To be sure you know whether someone is a true friend, take the Friendship Quiz.

Friendship Quiz

These are the names of 5 of my best friends, and the reasons I consider them to be loyal:

1. _____ because _____

34

2.		because	
3.		because	
4.		because	
5.		because	

Did it take you a long time to complete the "because" part for any of these friends? That may suggest you need to ask yourself these 5 Questions of Loyal Friendship:

1. Does she keep her dates with you, even if a guy wants to see her?

2. Does she make time for you, even though she has other friends?

3. If someone backstabs you, does she defend you?

4. Does she pressure you to do what she wants, even when she knows you're not interested?

5. Are you comfortable sharing your friend's behavior, both good and bad, with your parents?

What did you discover? Did you find that your so-called "friends" are often not there for you when you need them? Did you find that you've been giving more than you've been getting?

It's your *choice* (here's that word again) to decide which friends to keep around. This choosing process is called setting "boundaries."

What Are Boundaries?

Boundaries are imaginary fences we place around ourselves. They are the silent rules we follow to determine what is okay and what is not when it comes to relating to people. Boundaries are not meant to close people out, but to conserve your energy for clear-thinking independence.

Well-defined boundaries alert you when to say "no" and when to say "yes." They advise you about whom to hang out with. They instruct you to decline invitations when you have to study or when you're just too tired to go out. They tell you when you want to honor the need to stay home alone and just be quiet.

The beauty of boundaries is that we can draw these imaginary images in pencil, so we can erase them to let special people get closer. Because they are elastic, they allow us to expand our friendships after we've built a level of trust.

The great thing about boundary building is that we do this without having to answer to anyone. Boundaries are solely ours. They protect us. If we don't feel like getting too close to someone too quickly, it's okay. We can wait until we are ready to alter or expand the lines we have created.

<u>Gilda-Gram®</u>
**When you know how to set boundaries
with girlfriends,
you'll know how to set boundaries
with guys.**

So, think of your friendships with your girlfriends as learning experiences in how to deal with guys. Practice following the "5 Questions of Loyal Friendship," stick to your values without backing down, and remember you deserve to be treated well by *everyone* you meet, both girls and guys.

WANT #2

A Cool Boyfriend

A new product had just arrived on the market. It was a $3 pack of nine trading cards called "Boy Crazy!" It consisted of pictures of cute boys along with some of their traits, like age, eye color, horoscope sign, and the type of girls they prefer. There was a web site that accompanied the cards, and on it, girls registered to vote for a boy of the week to host a live chat.

Even before the cards became commercially available, 47,000 girls had already registered. There is no question that most teen girls want to find a cool boyfriend. But why do girls have so many problems achieving this goal? I believe it's because girls have a misconception of what life and love are all about.

Dump the Fairy Tale Mentality

Remember the fairy tales that were read to you when you were a little girl? From so many stories, girls learned that love came as a result of waiting. Snow White, Sleeping Beauty, and Cinderella all met princes who were not quite "ready" for commitment. So these guys went off on their different journeys to seek adventure. Eventually, they came home to the gals who were either pining for them, locked in a castle tower, or deadened in a deep sleep.

While entertaining, these fairy tales did girls a disservice. Girls learned that the most important thing for a girl is to find a "prince." The fairy tale girls did nothing productive while their guys were away. But miraculously, after the princes reappeared and kissed them or carried off the patient ladies, everyone woke up and lived "happily ever after."

So our fairy tales implied, "Even though he's out partying, girls, your job is to wait around, go to sleep for a few years, and your dreams on hold. Your life will only count when *he* says it can."

Okay, we know "happily ever after" doesn't exist. If they did, there would not be so many divorces. In reality, even the best relationships have ups and downs that need to be worked through.

Nonetheless, girls are taught they must kiss a lot of frogs before they find that one prince. Even parents who have tried to raise their daughters with a reality check constantly run into this myth.

My friend took her innocent four-year-old daughter on a camping trip with her older sister's brownie troop. Before my friend knew it, little Melissa was holding a dirty frog in the palm of her hand.

My friend appreciates cleanliness, so she screamed, "Melissa, put that filthy thing down." But Melissa yelled, "No, Mom, I can't. I want to kiss him now so he'll turn into a handsome prince." And with that she smacked one on the little creature.

You would think this child would have realized that since the frog remained a frog, the kiss idea was only make believe. But Melissa went on and on the whole evening, telling her mom that someday her prince would truly come—because she kissed the frog!

Little girls who believe a prince will find them and sweep them into a cloud of romance grow into adult women who believe that someday *their* prince will come, too. I've had 20-year-olds seriously ask me, "You mean there's no Prince Charming?"

When we imagine that guys have royal qualities, we encourage them to think they're more than human. We put them on a pedestal, allow them to treat us badly, and we give in to pressures we don't need and can't handle. Like little Melissa, we think the frog is a prince in disguise, and he'll suddenly surprise us with love.

Girls, let's dump our fairy tale mentality and get real. We need to see guys as mortal, imperfect humans. Then,

1. We won't feel shy about talking to guys because we'll know they're just like us.

2. We won't allow them to make us feel bad
   because we'll know how to expect respect.

When people are our real friends, they treat us well. Friends look out for each other. They cover our back. They go out of their way not to hurt our feelings. When we treat guys as our equals, rather than supermen, they return the respect we give them.

<u>Gilda-Gram®</u>
To have a cool boyfriend,
dump the fairy tale mentality
and get real.

<u>Success Makes You Beautiful</u>

Today, most young women recognize they deserve to have dreams. They know they have a right to pursue them and they must strive to succeed. More enlightened girls get good educations to position themselves to become financially secure so as not to depend on a guy to support them.

However, no matter how much money they're earning, too many young women still base their happiness on whether they have a guy. Years ago, Ally McBeal was the star character on one of the hottest shows on TV. Even though she had a law degree and a great job, her entire life revolved around trying to connect with a guy to get married and have babies. Translation: "Despite my scholastic achievements and my successful career, I'm still nothing without a man."

With her desperate "Gotta-Get-a-Husband" attitude, it was a miracle she kept her job as a lawyer! In the real world, she wouldn't. But because of the popularity of this TV show, we saw many gullible girls behaving like Ally McBeal.

This show was not the only TV role model that instructed girls that hooking up is the most important thing in life. Another media icon was Felicity. She chose to reject high-ranking Stanford University, so she could follow her crush to a less-prestigious New York City university! Although outrageous, girls flocked to watch this weekly TV show, too.

College is where a girl spends four years of her life supposedly improving herself. Not Felicity. As an incoming freshman, she had already selected her major to be "guy-chasing." A wise 26-year-old male recently told me, "Girls give up too much to be with guys. And guys don't respect them for it." WOW!

Guys who are chased by needy chicks are turned off. What we don't see in movies is that a girl's desperation to find a guy, get married, and have babies is as appealing to a guy as a cold shower.

Boyfriends come and go, but your dreams, goals, and how you prepare to meet them are yours forever. Girls must stick to their dreams. And crush craving should not be one of them.

Gilda-Gram®
You GOAL, girl!

And here's a big secret a lot of girls don't know:
When you make your main goal improving *yourself*,
guys find you more attractive.

Love's Disappointments

Girls who have avoided pursuing their own
passions are especially shattered when a guy leaves
them. Angie is a 13-year-old in the eighth grade. As a
pretty blonde soccer player, she's probably the most
popular girl in her school. She had been going with her
boyfriend, Brian, for three months.

Suddenly, one of her friends called to say that
Brian wanted to break up with her. Then came another
call from another girl who said the same thing. This
time, Angie asked why. The second friend told her that
Brian thought it was getting too serious.

The friends recounted the times Angie had been
with her boyfriend. They reviewed the unwritten junior
high bible they called "The Code." The Code consists of
the four sexual bases based on the baseball game: first
base, French kiss; second base, a boy feels under a girl's
shirt; third base, a girl feels down a guy's pants; home
base, intercourse.

Angie and her friend discussed how she had

finally agreed to go to second base with Brian. However, the next time they were together, she d her mind and refused. A couple of days later, he chose to break up with her.

Angie was so popular, she didn't care that Brian ended their relationship. But she did care *why* he did it. Fortunately, Angie has enough hobbies to keep her mind off this jerk.

Girls without hobbies or interests other than guys fall to pieces when they're dumped, because they have nowhere to go to get relief.

Disappointing love is why Alice, below, feels the way she does.

Dear Dr. Gilda,
        Doc, sorry to tell ya this, but I doubt I'm the first. Love sucks!!!
Alice

Young Alice is already aware of the pitfalls of losing your heart to someone. In reality, how can love "suck" when being in love is meant to feel great?

Eighteen-year-old Christine recently told me, "I've seen my mom and dad get divorced. During her breakup, my mom said that she never wanted to be without a man. So she hooked up with a guy only six weeks after her split with my father. She's now remarried--and I don't think she's happy. Actually, I don't see any point in ever getting married."

Yet Christine admits she wouldn't mind finding a cool guy with whom to have a short-term relationship. But having a permanent commitment is something she never wants. She figures, "Why should I set myself up for letdown?"

I told Christine that quick relationships are often followed by painful splits. Who needs the heartache of constant breakups? Serial relationships can be prevented if you find someone from the start who won't disappoint you.

My Guy is Cool
--But Is He Cool for *Me*?

By "cool," I mean someone that cares enough about you to cover your back! Teen girls are wising up. The Centers for Disease Control has thankfully seen a falling teen birth rate for 15 to 19-year-olds since 1996. Those stats suggest girls are becoming more responsible, despite what their own hormones might want to do.

Hormones also get you to change your mind a lot about whether a guy is right for you. (Another reason not to become a young mommy.) After being with one guy for a while, many young women question whether they even want to stay with him.

Dear Dr. Gilda,
My boyfriend is a really sweet guy, like the type mom and dad dream I'll bring home. However, at times

he's very immature. Every day, I go through a list of
questions, asking myself whether I should stay with him
or break it off.

There are more Cons than Pros. We've been
together for 4 months. What should I do? Please, please
help me!
A Dear Fan

Dear A Dear Fan,
No guy will ever have 100 percent of the
qualities you'd like. (And by the way, princess, you'll
never have 100 percent of the qualities he'd like, either.)
Complete my "Make-a-Choice Quiz," and I think you'll
be closer to figuring this out. Let me know what you
find.
Dr. Gilda

Make-A-Choice Quiz

Create two lists showing the Pros and Cons of
staying with your boyfriend. After you have written as
many Pros and Cons as you can think of, assign a
number from 1 to 5 to each item you listed, 1 being the
Least Important to you, and 5 being the Most Important.

When you're finished, add the scores you got in
the Pros list, and the scores you got in the Cons list.
Your numbers will tell you which of the two lists is
more meaningful to you. Then all you have to do is act
on the information you've discovered about yourself.

Here's Marsha's list for her boyfriend of six months:

PROs

4   He's very affectionate when we're alone.

4   He goes out of his way to do little things for me.

3   He makes me laugh.

4   He treats me with respect in front my friends.

CONs

5   He ignores me when he's with his friends.

5   Sometimes he doesn't call me for days.

3   He often tries to make me jealous.

5   He doesn't tell people he has a girlfriend.

2   He rarely invites me when he goes to places with his friends.

Marsha's Pros totaled 15. Her Cons totaled 20. Obviously, the Cons won. From this, she concluded her boyfriend was upsetting her more than she even realized. At first, she didn't want to accept the truth. But when we talked about it, she said that of all the Cons she listed, she was especially upset after her guy would sweet-talk her with a promise to call the next day, and not keep his word.

To make her list come out better, she tried

47

desperately to think of more Pros to write, but she was stumped. This quiz showed her it was time to look at whether this guy was good for her. Her heart knew the answer.

Sadly, she chose to say goodbye, and seek someone who had her best interests, someone who had back.

Gilda-Gram®
**Deep down, we all know
what's best for us.**

If you're ambivalent about whether a guy is right for you, take the "Make-a-Choice Quiz." Then you'll see the obvious.

When a girl decides what to do, she must stick to her boundaries. Her commitment to her boundaries is very appealing to cool guys. It shows them she thinks for herself and is not easily swayed. That's a challenge cool boys enjoy.

When a guy knows his girl is independent, and is with him only because she chooses to be, he feels great about winning her heart. There are plenty of girls too willing to take any guy, just to have a boyfriend. But if your behavior projects that you are choosy, and you'll only be with a guy you think is terrific, your boyfriend will be pleased to have the rep of being your special man.

In addition, his friends will think that since he's won your heart, he *must* be cool. Guys love it when their buddies think they're cool.

If you're still uncertain about whether to make your man a keeper, examine "A Cool Guy's Traits," below. Of the 30 traits listed, check out whether your current crush--or even one in your past had enough of these characteristics to make you happy.

A Cool Guy's Traits

1. Is he 100 percent committed to you?

2. Does he make you a priority?

3. Does he aim to make you happy?

4. Is he optimistic about life?

8. Does he accept you as you are?

9. Do you share common interests?

10. Do you share a similar sense of humor?

11 Does he confide in you?

12. Does he consider your feelings?

13. Does he keep his promises--like calling when he says he will?

14. Is he independent?

15. Does he handle his disappointments well?

16. Does he tell you the truth?

17. Does he admit when he's wrong?

18. Does he inconvenience himself for you?

19. Is he respectful to your friends and family?

20. Is he proud of you?

21. Does he set and pursue his goals?

22. Is he generous toward you?

23. Does he have respectful friends?

24. Does he make his own decisions?

25. Does he compliment you?

26. Does he have a strong bond with his mom?

27. Does he introduce you to his friends, and speak highly of you to others?

28. Does he respect your need to work on a project, be with your friends, or just veg out alone?

29. Does he show interest in an activity you love?

30. Does he show you affection?

This list will explain why an old relationship went sour. It will also alert you, before you detour down a seedy relationship road.

<u>**Gilda-Gram®**</u>
A cool guy is as supportive as a good bra.

Do You Think These Guys Are Cool?

Here is an email from a girl who had not yet taken the "Make-a-Choice Quiz," or read "A Cool Guy's Traits." Based on what you know now, would you call these guys "cool"--and worth keeping?

Dear Dr. Gilda,

I have a very big problem with this guy. We've seen each other for over a year, but he never asks me out. We never have a real conversation and he never asks me anything about my life, like how is school going. He never invites me to the parties he throws, he rarely calls me on the phone, and it seems like all he wants to get from me is sex. I was so naive I gave it to him. He told me twice he loved me.

The first time was at the park. He was holding me tight in his arms. At the time, I was cheating on my boyfriend, and I guess he wanted me only for himself. He convinced me he loved me when he looked in my eyes and said those 3 words I didn't expect.

I was confused, because I didn't know who to choose, my then-boyfriend or this guy. So I didn't say "I love you" back. I guess that made him feel bad.

The second time he said "I love you" was after having sex with me for the first time. I was the one who said it first.

My problem now is that I can't stop thinking about him. I can't concentrate on school. I get so mad and jealous when he flirts with other girls I want to beat them up. I feel offended every time he makes fun of me or says bad things about me. Even though he treats me like crap, I always end up falling for him.

If he spit in my face, I would still take him back. I've told myself so many times this past year that he's not boyfriend material. But it doesn't click in my head. When I ignore him, he ends up coming back. I always think he will eventually change, but it never happens.

I'm tired of all this bullcrap, but I still think I'm in love and these feelings will never go away. I think it's impossible for me to find a guy who will respect me and love me for who I am, not for my looks. I want to be with him. What should I do?
Soft Lips

I sent Soft Lips the "Make-a-Choice Quiz," and "A Cool Guy's Traits." Also, I responded with this note:

Dear Soft Lips,
This guy is playing you for a fool and you know it. I'm sending you two of my assessment tools.

The first requires you to list your guy's Pros and Cons, and then weigh them according to what you find important. This way, you can see what you really think you want in a cool guy. The second lists 30 cool traits a keeper should have.

After you have completed these assessments, please send me your results.
Dr. Gilda

Soft lips must really have been hurting because she answered my email within hours. She wrote:

Dear Dr. Gilda,

These were the best quizzes I ever took! The "Make-a-Choice Quiz" showed me information I could not have gotten anywhere else. In fact, both quizzes made me come face-to-face with facts I didn't want to deal with. After I completed them, I cried. These were my results:

PROs

___3___ I like calling this guy my boyfriend, because he's very popular and it makes me feel popular, too.

___5___ When we have sex, I feel loved.

___3___ I have to admit that the challenge of whether he'll be around is exciting.

CONs

___5___ We never have a real conversation.

___5___ He never asks me anything about my life.

___5___ The only time he calls me is to set up a date for sex.

___5___ He's taken my mind off school, and my grades are failing.

___5___ He flirts with other girls in front of me.   '

___4___ My problems with him have affected my relationships with others.

____4____ I know he doesn't respect me or care about what happens to me.

Soft Lips' PROs totaled 11, but her CONs totaled an overwhelming 33. Now she clearly saw how destructive her relationship with this guy was.

She also saw that the PROs she thought were important to her were lightweights compared to the seriousness of the CONs she wrote.

But Soft Lips didn't stop there. She went on to examine "A Cool Guy's Traits." She said that's when her tears really came pouring out.

As she went down the List, beginning with the first item—"Is he 100 percent committed to you?"--she answered "No," "No," "No," to each of the 30 statements. At first, she didn't believe that boyfriends could ever behave nicely to their girls. Then, finally, she recognized there are guys who are respectful. There are guys who care about the girls they're with. There are guys who are supportive of the girls they're with.

Soft Lips admitted, "I have not gone after any of these guys. Maybe I didn't think I could find a guy who will always respect me and love me for who I am, not for my looks."

She also admitted that when she became jealous, because of her roving-eyed Romeo, it was not the other girls who were at fault. She had to abandon the idea of beating them up. She finally got it that the only person she had to work on was *her*.

This new information provided a rude awakening for Soft Lips, and she wouldn't stop thanking me.

Recently, I received a note from this young woman, along with her photo. Yes, she really was gorgeous. Standing next to her was a tall, handsome guy who looked like he adored her. Her note said, "Finally, I found a cool guy. This one's got my back— and I feel very secure with him." Hooray for Soft Lips!

Cool guys DO exist. They don't set out to give a girl a hard time. They're comfortable with being themselves, they're not afraid to show their emotions, and they're happy to be loving and respectful.

Someone is going to be a girlfriend to one of these cool guys, so why can't it be you? To be the girlfriend of a cool guy, all you have to do is know what you need. This is not so hard. Discover your needs in Part II.

PART II

WHAT EVERY GIRL *NEEDS*

<u>NEED #1</u>

Be an *It Girl*

Being an *It Girl* puts the spotlight entirely on you. You know you've got a lot going for you, and you don't misbelieve you need a guy's breath to give you life.

<u>Gilda-Gram®</u>
He's not all that!
YOU are!!

Many girls go gaga over a so-so guy and think they're in love. Before they know it, they're ready to fly to the moon to be with Mr. Wonderful. They give up doing the things that make them happy, they leave their friends, they ignore their parents, and they generally "drop out" of the life they used to know.

These desperate girls are always available to their guy, while he continues his life according to *his* plans. If this sounds absurd, read these sad letters.

Dear Dr. Gilda,

My boyfriend is in college and I am still in high school. It seems to be working out. I miss him, and my grades are slipping because all I think about is what we are going to do next weekend we'll be together. Yet when we're together, we never know what to do. When we do things we have already done, we get bored. Please help!
Louise

Dear Louise,

You say this relationship "seems to be working out," but you're wrong. Your guy's away pursuing his future, and you're letting your grades and goals slip through your fingers. How is this working out??

When the two of you finally do meet, you are bored. Your relationship is in trouble! But more importantly, after the two of you part, your poor grades won't get you into a decent college. So what will you have then?

Relationships are meant to *support* you, not drag you down. Start loving yourself more than you love your boyfriend. Otherwise, you'll be without a boyfriend *and* without a future of your own.
Dr. Gilda

Guys love It Girls who love themselves. Your girl power oozes when you know you have what it takes. Extroverted It Girls become an entire party, larger than life. Introverted It Girls demonstrate confidence that shows they know who they are more quietly.

Just recently, within a span of two weeks I met

two *very* cool guys in their late 20's. Each is quite different from the other. One is a handsome white news anchor on a popular TV channel in New York. The other is a gorgeous black politician who runs a government program for inner city kids in California.

Both these guys dated the most beautiful women in their cities. Both were confirmed bachelors who refused to commit to any one woman, despite the constant flow of ladies chasing them.

But now both guys fell in love with someone they intend to marry. I asked each one what made their special woman different from the others. Each guy confided, "My girlfriend has a better sense of who she is than any other woman I know." That says everything for It Girls!!

Somehow, a lot of females either don't feel confident enough about who they are, or they only feel good about themselves if they have a boyfriend. Psychologist Dr. Joyce Brothers said a man falls in love at least seven times before he finds the one he wants to spend his life with.

Unfortunately, most girls enter relationships thinking they are going to be "the one" a guy will love forever. These girls act desperate, and pounce on the first guy who comes along, as long as he's breathing.

Dear Dr. Gilda,

Please help. I need a boyfriend! I just can't get the one I'm crushing over! I don't know what to do! I always try to get myself to talk to him, but it just doesn't

happen! It would look really weird if I just went over and spoke to him! Please help!
Crushing in New York

Notice all those exclamation points!!! Would you rate Crushing in New York as *mildly interested* in finding a boyfriend or *gotta-hook-up-fast desperate*?

I think it's clear that Crushing wants a boyfriend so badly she'd do anything to get one. Guys pick up desperate vibes. No guy feels good about a girl who wants to have *any* boy, rather than a *special* boy. So the first thing Crushing has to do is calm down! That won't be easy, if she continues to beg for love.

> <u>6-year-old</u>: "I'm in love with Fred, and he loves me more than anyone else in the whole wide world."
>
> <u>Mother</u>: "Are you going to marry Fred?"
>
> <u>6-year-old</u>: "No, he's got hot hands."

While this 6-year-old thinks she loves Fred "more than anyone else in the whole wide world," she also realizes she won't marry him because he has this fatal flaw. It's good to see she's so picky at her early age, but the flaw she mentions is a superficial one. She doesn't talk about not marrying Fred because he's mean to her. Young women are often similar to this 6-year-old in choosing superficial traits rather than those that matter!

Dear Dr. Gilda,
My boyfriend and I just got engaged. I love him

to death, but we fight all the time. My mother and father have been remarried 4 times each. I don't want this to happen to me. I don't know if I can handle it any more.

I go to school full time and work full time, just to get away. I don't know what I would do without him, though. I support him mentally, physically, and financially. I would do anything for him. I know he loves me a lot, but I just wish he would show it.

How do I get him to be less jealous and more affectionate? I want to be able to go out with my friends without him getting mad. I want a healthy relationship. How do I make it work? I know communication is key. But he gets mad when I mention this stuff, and we end up fighting more.
Tiffany

Dear, dear Tiffany,

If you're not happy with your boyfriend now, things will only get worse as life becomes more complex. You are right that communication is key to every relationship. If your guy blows up, or even blows you off when you raise an issue he doesn't like, that's a warning he can't communicate well. And it's also a good indicator of how he'll remain.

You say you don't know what you would do without him. But you are carrying the burden of the relationship, by supporting him "mentally, physically, and financially." How is he looking out for you?

He's jealous, he doesn't show you enough affection, and he allows you to do all the relationship work. You ask how *you* can make it work.

You two are not candidates for marriage at this time. If you intend to remain engaged, seek counseling before you plan a wedding. Sort out how you interpret the marriages of your mom and dad. Running away from your upbringing to a job or marriage is not a solution. Don't let that happen!
Dr. Gilda

When a girl feels bad in love, the problem is usually that she has put too much faith in the myth that her guy will take her to happily-ever-after land. Tiffany is trying too hard to maintain this relationship single-handedly. And how does her guy re-pay her? With jealousy, control, and arguments.

Sadly, Tiffany wants love so badly, she accepts nasty behavior from her guy, becomes engaged to him, and considers spending her life like this. NO!

Gilda-Gram®
**Don't be so needy to have *somebody*,
that you end up choosing *anybody*.**

Dear Dr. Gilda,
I really need some advice on how to find that "sweet" guy I can relate to. I've been meeting guys I have nothing in common with. My life is pretty complicated with a lot of problems, and I just want someone who will make me happy. Please help.
Amy

It's a bad idea for any girl to think she can get her happiness from a guy. Amy's looking for a boyfriend who will be a bandage for her "complicated problems." Guys have their own problems, and they would love to find someone to make *them* happy, not the other way around.

Girls looking for guys to rescue them should return to fairyland, sit by the cinders, and wait for the handsome prince to find their correct slipper size! When that doesn't happen, a girl better know how to shop for slippers on her own. An alleged "prince" can leave at any time.

Girls Who Accept "Less-Than" Treatment

Girls like Tiffany and Amy who expect their boyfriends to be *all that* often accept what I call "Less-Than" Treatment.

Gilda-Gram®
**"Less-Than" Treatment is treatment
that's *less than* okay.**

Girls who fall into this category believe there's truth in the title of an old Britney Spears' album, "Born to Make You Happy." They are the girls whose boyfriends buy them cell phones to know their whereabouts every hour of the day. They are the girls who only feel happy when they have a boyfriend. Should the boyfriend break up with them, they insist it's their fault. These girls put their guy on a pedestal and make him feel he can do no wrong.

Carolyn was in a relationship—sort of—with Tony for four months. Before long, she learned he was already with a long-term girlfriend, and she was his dish on the side.

For some reason, Carolyn decided to put up with Tony's antics. She said, "I love him a lot. He is my life and I don't know what I would do without him." Saying he was *her life* was Carolyn's first mistake. The only person who is your life is YOU.

Carolyn rationalized to her friends, "He's still with this girlfriend, trying to see how things will work out since he lives in one state and she lives in another. They never see each other, so I don't think they have much of a chance together."

She continued with him for another four months, even though it was upsetting her that he wasn't hers. She refused dates with other guys, although her friends tried to talk sense into her. She defended, "If things don't work out for him and his girlfriend, he will come to me because he loves me."

Carolyn's second mistake was her willingness to accept "Less-Than" Treatment by waiting around, putting her love life on hold, and accepting crumbs from a guy who couldn't decide if he wanted her. Even if Tony returns girlfriend-free, Carolyn still can't win because

Gilda-Gram®
What you accept, you teach

She's *accepted* his crummy behavior for so long, she *taught* him it would be okay if he ever wants to stray again. In his mind, she'd wait around indefinitely.

Unless there are seven little dwarfs she can live with until he comes around, the story sounds like a page from a fairy tale. All Carolyn would have to do to make this myth complete is to go to sleep--which she seems to be doing anyway as she waits. This couple can't possibly have a future.

Carolyn's third mistake was not to believe she is somebody. Any woman who thinks well of herself would never agree to put her life on hold for a dude.

A lot of girls don't have enough self-confidence to believe they deserve more. This was the situation Mindy also found herself in.

Dear Dr. Gilda,

I always wanted to be somebody. If I couldn't be somebody, I'd date someone who was somebody. So I went out with a lot of popular boys at school. After I graduated, I sought guys who had great jobs or who were big sports stars in my town.

The problem was that these guys were so into themselves they never cared about me. I'm miserable because I can't find anyone who loves me. I want to meet someone who really cares. What should I do?
Mindy

Ladies, your goal is always to find a guy who's got your back! Mindy is a typical young woman desiring love. But she's looking to get it from guys who are bad choices. Males who think they're *all that* come on like roaring lions. But deep down, they usually have low self-esteem, which they cover up with conceit. Their fragile egos are so big, they have no room for a girlfriend.

Girls who are attracted to *all that*-type guys are forever feeling let down. Like Mindy, girls who attract guys with low self-esteem lack self-esteem themselves. The proof of Mindy's shabby self-image is found in the second sentence of her email: "If I couldn't be somebody, I'd date someone who was somebody." Whether or not we'd admit it, we attract guys who are like us.

This is how it works. You don't believe you're special enough to attract a cool guy. So your body language, voice, and words project an image that screams you're not valuable. You draw people to you who reinforce the negative way you feel about yourself. If a girl with low self-image were to somehow attract a hotshot guy, she'd think something is wrong with him for wanting *her*.

It's amazing how other people automatically "read" your cues without having to ask you directly whether your self-esteem is high or low. These cues are totally designed by you. No guy can raise or lower the way you feel about yourself--unless you give him permission.

In an old movie, "In and Out," the main character admits he's gay, right before his wedding. His bride-to-be becomes hysterical. She reveals her self-esteem was based on his willingness to marry her. "I thought you could make me feel like a beautiful woman, instead of the girl nobody wanted," she wails.

Although this movie is a comedy, like Mindy, the character felt she could only become somebody *by connecting to a* guy. No *prince* will awaken you from your deep snooze and breathe life into you. The idea of expecting a guy to give *your* life meaning is a shaky foundation for love.

At first, a guy is flattered by a girl who credits him for being *all that*. But eventually, he grows tired of carrying the burden of *her* life around with his own. Guys like women who are intelligent and have an independent life they enjoy.

If you think a boyfriend should live your life for you, here's a flash: Most guys believe that's too much pressure, and will leave a girl like you. There are no free rides. Every male and female must pull his or her own weight.

Remember those two great guys who fell in love with two women who thought highly of themselves? These guys will be forever excited and challenged by their ladies who are not shy about speaking their mind and relaying their feelings.

Cool guys might complain their new girls are "high maintenance." But these guys show their It Girls utmost respect.

Gilda-Gram®
Respect is what keeps love alive.

In just a few years of dating, Mindy has learned that the guys she's been attracting are not good for her. Now she's faced with the challenge of attracting a different sort of guy. What should she do when all along she's only liked the type who caused her pain?

This has nothing to do with the *guys'* flaws. It has to do with Mindy herself. She's got to change her guy radar. Before concentrating on having a romance with a *guy*, she must seek a romance with *herself*. Mindy must learn she can surely be somebody, without a boost from a boyfriend.

Gilda-Gram®
No guy can rev your engine
as well as you can.

What if you fell for a guy who was so "sweet" -- except for one small problem--his girlfriend?

Dear Dr. Gilda,

I am a 22-year-old female and I'm dating a 23-year-old guy. He's very sweet, and he calls me nearly 5 times a day, and visits me whenever he can. He even writes me letters and poems, saying he's starting to fall in love with me. I'm falling for him, too.

The only problem is that he recently told me that he's kinda in another relationship. He lives with her and she picks him up from work every day. He told me he doesn't like her and they argue all the time.

He says he wants to be with me and he can see us getting married. But going out with him and being intimate is bothering me, because afterwards he goes home to her bed. I really like him and I don't know what to do.
Marla

Dear Marla,
You say he's "kinda in another relationship," which you then explain as an out-and-out living arrangement with another woman!! Open your eyes! This couple is so close she even picks him up from work.

Break off all ties with this two-timer. Not only is he not emotionally available, he also wants an insurance policy that you'll be there for him *if* he leaves his girlfriend. That's a big "if." If you gave him the brush-off, he'd continue living where he is because he fears being on his own. That translates to his being a BIG BABY!!

Don't fall for the nonsense that he doesn't like her and that all they do is argue. He's looking for a mommy, and if his live-in won't do, maybe you can take her place.

You're right to be miserable about his cheating. Since he's living with one woman while romancing another, he will easily do the same to you. Tell him to get a life—out of yours. You need a grownup man.

Dr. Gilda

Marla and all the girls like her should recognize that having *no* guy is better than being with a two-timer.

Marla's not alone. I get thousands of emails from young women who like attached, unavailable men who promise they're going to dump their ladies, stop living with them, or get divorced.

Gilda-Gram®
No matter what a guy tells you,
only his *actions* tell the truth.

Dear Dr. Gilda,
I started talking to my best friend's cousin, without knowing he had a girlfriend. Now I find he not only has a girlfriend, but he also lives with her. I am only 17, and he's 24. But I started to have very strong feelings for him. I feel kind of bad because when she goes to work, I am in her house.

He's the person I've been looking for. He makes me feel things I never felt before. I know I'm young, but I have never had these feelings before about anyone. He keeps saying he's going to move out, but he hasn't.

My friends call me a home wrecker. I don't feel I am because this guy and his girlfriend had problems before I came into the picture. Please help!
Chauna

Dear Chauna,
I know it feels great to have an older guy interested in you. It also feels great to think he'd leave

his girlfriend for you. But this guy's a dog for leading you on while he's living with his girlfriend. He has some nerve to have you over there. This is outright disrespect for this girl and for their relationship--whether he intends to remain there or leave.

Even if this dog goes off with you, will you trust him not to do the same thing to you? Sure, you could be called a home wrecker. I'd also call you "gullible." Whether or not this couple had problems before you entered the picture is irrelevant. He has some nerve telling you their private business. How'd you like to *be* this girlfriend?

What goes around comes around. If you're the in-between person now, you could end up having someone in between you and your next guy. Leave this dude! Tell yourself--and him-- you deserve more. Then go get it!
Dr. Gilda

Believing you deserve the full enchilada is what being an It Girl is all about. An It Girl knows--not merely *thinks*--that she is terrific and worthy, and she projects that knowledge to each guy she meets.

Look at Mindy's letter again. She says, "If I couldn't be somebody..." Hey, Mindy and Chauna and Carolyn and Amy, and all the young women who resemble them, there's no "if" about it; **everyone *is* somebody.** And you should also know that everybody who's somebody probably once began feeling like nobody--until they learned these skills.

Get your It Girl gear on. Lavish yourself with the same kind of attention *Mr. All That* lavishes on himself. Go out and do the things you love. Buy that outfit you've been longing for. Study passionately for that upcoming test—and reward yourself later for acing it!

Discover that the sense of accomplishment you get from meeting your goals is amazing. If your new ego-massage doesn't feel comfortable at first, keep it going until you get used to it. Once you begin to enjoy your own super treatment, you'll wonder why you hadn't begun it sooner.

When someone knows she's somebody, her positive thoughts become guy magnets.

Gilda-Gram®
**If you want to improve your lovelife,
love your life.**

Instead of being a spectator, get out and *do*! The more exciting things you *do*, the more exciting people you'll meet.

Gilda-Gram®
**If you want love that won't keep letting you down,
don't keep letting yourself down.**

Feeling you're somebody is a necessity, not a luxury. Whether they're outwardly bold, or strongly silent, It Girls think so highly of themselves they create a buzz others want to be around.

When I was teaching junior high kids, I found a poster I hung in my classroom. It said: "I know I'm somebody 'cause God don't make no junk." My students asked for copies to take home. I had taught them that self-pride would provide great success.

Girls Who Don't Think They're Somebody

Plenty of women don't think they're somebody. That's why it's important to learn the skills of somebody-building now. Read this disturbing letter from a high school senior married for just six months.

Dear Dr Gilda,

I am very sad because my husband cheated on me in front of my face. See, my husband wanted to be in a multiple person sexual situation, which I agreed to. We did this with my best friend and his wife. My best friend and I were way too close to even think of touching each other. So we just stopped and laughed.

However, my husband continued going with his wife. My best friend and I even walked out of the room, and they still kept going. My husband does not understand why I am upset. Do I have a right to be upset? Please help me.
June

The next-to-last sentence is especially disturbing: "Do I have a right to be upset?" Only a girl who doesn't think she's somebody would ask if she has the *right* to feel.

Young women who have not had enough experience living should not be committing themselves to life-long ties. Even movie stars make this mistake. Drew Barrymore married a bar owner at 19, and divorced him only two months later. Milla Jovovich, married an actor at 17, and divorced him after her mom had it annulled. She was then married again at 22, to a director, and divorced at 24. Jennie Garth married a musician at 22, and divorced two years later, just seven months before giving birth to another guy's baby.

Girls Who *Know* They're Somebody

A study at Lafayette College found that very smart students are often teased for being gifted. While boys often fend off negative reactions by becoming the class clown, girls tend to deny their intelligence.

While "dumbing down" may seem to allow girls to fit in, these young women are learning to limit their potential by lying about whom they are. People who live a lie consistently bury their wit, feelings, and social skills.

Every girl has not only a right to her feelings, but an obligation to express them. Girls who express that they're somebody are called "It Girls" for a reason. It Girls don't believe they're *all that*. *All that* types are conceited and cocky. It Girls know they're popular, understand they're smart, and are not afraid to show it. They feel they're cool, and they love life.

When it comes to guys, they would rather not be

with *just anyone* for the *wrong* reasons. They'd rather be *alone* for the *right* ones.

It Girls confront people who try to take advantage of them. Just the way they carry themselves sends the message, "You want me to do what? I don't think so." So these girls are not even approached to compromise their values. And guys know these girls will never accept being their doormats.

How to Become an It Girl

What gives an It Girl her "Itness"? The answer is confidence. Confidence is the faith you have in yourself that lets everyone know you have unshakeable self-respect. To respect someone is to accept her. An It Girl's self-respect shows she likes herself and she feels secure about the person she is.

Feeling Secure vs. Feeling Significant

Secure girls feel happy about *whom they are*, as opposed to *what they do*. Despite the stupid mistakes they make each day (who doesn't?), they're still glad to be who they are. Secure girls don't compare themselves to others. An It Girl's s*ecurity* comes from within.

Feeling secure protects the It Girl, even when she has those negative feelings and occasional bouts of self-doubt, which everyone experiences from time to time. But because those doubts are inside her, her body guards her security, and no one has the power to shatter it.

An It Girl feels secure about whom she is, despite whether she questions what to do about her boyfriend.

Dear Dr. Gilda,

During my first year in high school, I met this cute guy. I was curious about him, and became his friend. It turned out that he is one of the friendliest, sweetest, and most charming people I know. We have become incredibly good friends. We talk about any thing, any time.

I have realized that my initial infatuation has now turned to real caring and warm feelings. After graduation, I went to college, and now we're 500 miles apart. We still keep in touch, and on my occasional trips to his area, we always go out. When he has a chance, he visits me, too.

Should I risk this beautiful friendship by disclosing I care for him more than as a friend? Or should I wait?
Carrie

Dear Carrie,

I receive many questions like yours about when and how to act on a friendship that's developing into love. The difference between your question and the others I get is that you and your guy have spent at least four years getting to know each other.

I believe your question is more about timing than it is about whether you stand a chance. When you feel most comfortable, gently ask him where he thinks your relationship is going. Let him talk freely.

From what he says--and doesn't say--and the way he looks at you and touches you when he says it, you'll know.

From the sound of your email, there's a lot happening between you, but it just hasn't yet been stated. After all this time, raise the question. Please let me know his response.
Dr. Gilda

When a girl is *secure*, she doesn't feel at risk about asking a guy what's up. If he responds, "There's nothing more than friendship," she'll be hurt and disappointed, but she'll continue feeling good about herself, even if it means being without him.

Test your feelings of security. You are wearing a new outfit. No one has complimented you on it all day. How do you react? Do you feel depressed or upset that no one noticed? Your answer may suggest you are uncertain about your feelings of worth, and you're in need of an outside source to justify you. Girls who feel secure *know* they're "It"!

In contrast to feelings of security, feelings of *significance* depend not on your confidence, but on how *competent* you feel with the externals around you. Therefore, significant feelings consist of what you achieve, which friends you have, and how situations affect you. These are changeable, so, unlike your security, your feelings of significance can alter.

If no one complimented your great new outfit,

you might feel *insignificant,* even though you still feel secure about who you are as a person.

Sometimes we're evaluated positively and sometimes we're not. The good thing about the changing feelings of significance is that once you remove yourself from negative surroundings, you can watch your competence---and significance--soar.

Do you think this woman is feeling insecure or insignificant?

Dear Dr. Gilda,
I have a problem with my boyfriend. I can't trust him anymore. He has been selling porn magazines on his school bus and at school. He said he got rid of them for me, but a little while later I saw him selling them again.

The only time we talk is on the phone, once or twice every two weeks. He doesn't look at me anymore, and I think it is because he'd rather look at naked women he doesn't know. My question is whether I should dump him.
Sari

Dear Sari,
You already know what to do. This guy makes you feel bad by not paying attention to you. Also, he's doing things you don't respect.

Dump him and attract someone who looks forward to being with you. While your so-called "boyfriend" drools over the make-believe images in the

magazines, you'll have a *real* guy who gives you what
you need.
Dr. Gilda

Sari doesn't feel significant around her
boyfriend, but she feels secure enough to understand
there is a problem. Dumping this dude would release
her insignificant feelings, although she's obviously not
looking forward to taking that step.

Because they're dependent on other people and
situations, feelings of significance can alter. If you get a
good grade in biology, you feel significant, but if you
get into a screaming match with your best friend, you
may not feel significant at all. You may still be secure
about who you are as a person, but this situation has
bummed you out.

Develop unchanging *internal* confidence,
knowing *external* confidence will alter depending on the
circumstance. Happily, your internal confidence will
handle external situations with grace.

Can Being an *It* Turn to (Sh)it?

I appeared on a TV talk show about teens who
dress too sexy. Deanna, 15, was a chubby girl who
walked on stage in a tiny skirt and tank top. As she
strutted past the other guests, she crowed, "I am super
cool."

The audience booed. She shot back, "I love
showing off my body. I have a great butt, chest, and

face. I can get any man I want. Anyone who has a problem with me is just jealous." The audience booed more.

Would you call Deanna confident or cocky? While I was doing a keynote speech for several hundred high school students, I asked, "What's the difference between being confident and cocky?" A girl responded, "When you're cocky, you have to tell everyone how great you are. When you're confident, all you have to do is show up; everyone will know you're great." Brilliant!

Deanna's cocky attitude turned people off. I explained on the TV show that confident people walk into a room with the attitude, "Here I am, world... now tell me about you." Cocky people walk into a room with the attitude, "Here I am, world... and who cares about you?" Cockiness is often a cover-up for feeling crappy, and it's the quality in guys you want to avoid.

Being confident is inviting. You feel good enough about yourself to invite others to share your feelings. You are anxious to give to others, and because of your caring attitude, others want to be around you.

Consider Deanna. Did she really think she was so great? As we got further into how she feels about herself *beneath* her clothes, she displayed a scared, insecure girl, looking to attract attention.

Gilda-Gram®
**Attracting *attention* is not
the same as attracting *love*.**

Deanna thought that by wearing revealing clothes, she'd get a guy to love her. When she revealed the poor quality of the guys she was luring, she left the show much wiser. Girls who have to say they're somebody don't feel great about themselves.

Gilda-Gram®
Less is more.

When you're somebody, *everyone knows!*

How Confident Are You?

How do you measure your confidence? You've heard about IQ, or Intelligence Quotient, the score used to gauge how smart you are. I've created a score for CQ, or Confidence Quotient, a measure to show if you really *believe* you're somebody. It Girls have a high CQ.

Since your aim is to strengthen your internal confidence, the questions on this quiz relate to the *security* of who you *are,* rather than to the *significance* of what you *do.* As with every other quiz in this book, there are no right or wrong answers. Your scores will show how you feel about yourself now.

What's My CQ (Confidence Quotient)?

Mark "T" for True or "F" for False after each statement:

1. I often blame my parents for the way my life is.

2. When I attract popular guys, it's not because of my charm, but because of my luck.

3. I often think, "I wish I were prettier."

4. I consider myself lame if I don't have at least one guy interested in me.

5. When a guy begins to like me, I assume it won't last.

6. I value how others think of me.

7. I'm not comfortable telling guys how I feel.

8. When I meet a new guy, I often think, "Why bother? He won't like me anyway."

9. I usually feel uncomfortable when people compliment me or give me gifts.

10. I rarely set goals for myself.

11. I prefer to belong to a popular crowd.

12. When I fail at something, I feel bad about myself.

13. I don't like myself a lot of the time.

14. When my friends criticize me I feel bad.

15. I often feel others are prettier, have more money, or are more popular than I am.

16. I don't make friends easily.

17. I don't want to hurt others' feelings by disagreeing with them.

18. I don't enjoy being alone.

19. I feel uncomfortable talking freely to others.

20. The thought of being bold is frightening.

ScoreCard

A high Confidence Quotient means you believe in yourself. If you had 3 or more Trues, your CQ needs a lift. When you believe in yourself, others will believe in you, especially the guys you want to attract.

What does a high CQ look like? Recently, parents were called to a Colorado school district, because hundreds of minors had been sexting nude photos of each other and voting on the best ones. The police got involved because even if the photos were consensual, the kids were minors and they could be arrested on child porn charges as sex offenders! That sentence would follow them for the rest of their lives! Do you think people who display naked photos of their bodies have high CQs?

Everyone feels insecure sometimes. At least, Frieda admits it openly. That's a start.

Dear Dr. Gilda,
On Halloween, my friend Jenny had a party and we were gonna go trick-or-treating together. She invited me and 4 other friends. We decided to dress in black, and put dark makeup on. We were having a blast. Jenny's cousin, Dallas, was over. He was playing video games, and we were ready to leave. When we got back, he was still there, and we ordered pizza and watched movies. Then he left, and the rest of us stayed the night.

My problem is that since that night, I have had a major crush on Dallas. I think about him a lot, and Jenny tells me he knows I like him. I'm not absolutely sure about that. She says she wants to talk to him and see if he will go out with me.

I don't have much confidence because I am overweight. I weigh 180 pounds, but my friends tell me I don't look THAT bad. I am totally afraid he won't like me, and that if I ever go to Jenny's again and he's there I will feel uncomfortable.

Dallas and I get along pretty well. We talk sometimes when I'm there and I know him pretty well. If my friend talks to him, what should she say? Is there anything I can do to get him to like me more? What if he thinks I am too fat? Help!
Frieda

Dear Frieda,

I've never liked the idea of one girl doing the talking for another. It's not Jenny's business to get you and Dallas together. If he's interested in you as a girlfriend he'll show you the signs.

More important than whether Dallas likes you, or whether he thinks you're too fat is the question of how you feel about yourself.

Dallas' presence in your mind is showing you have a problem with self-confidence, by your own admission. Make this an opportunity to make changes. Learn the traits of an It Girl, take the "CQ Test," and study how to boost your Confidence Quotient.

Girls who believe they're special find their extra pounds melt right off. Once you boost your self-confidence, you may be in a position of deciding whether *you* want *Dallas,* not the other way around!

Your issue is your self-confidence, not this guy's interest in you. Bump up the way you feel about YOU and watch your whole life improve.
Dr. Gilda

How Do I Raise My CQ?

After taking the last quiz, you may have discovered your CQ needs a jolt. To raise it, follow these 3 Steps: Believe, Conceive, Achieve.

Step #1
BELIEVE

Believing in yourself first requires that you recognize the payoffs of a high level of confidence. High CQ will attract boyfriends and girlfriends who are as confident as you. Notice that the It Girls in your school hang out with other It Girls. My Gilda-Gram® says, "We attract people who are like us."

Confident people feel good about themselves, and because they do, they are able to feel good about others without feeling jealous or envious. When people feel good about each other, they develop ties and become committed, the way The Little Prince became committed to the fox.

Visualize yourself at a party. You are dressed to impress. Imagine entering the room like you own it. Be friendly and strong. Stand tall and act perfectly in charge. Accept compliments gracefully. As soon as you believe in yourself, others will believe in you, too.

Step #2
CONCEIVE

The next step to raising your CQ is to conceive a plan to make it happen. Feeling confident doesn't just occur by itself. You must be determined to work at it. Vow you'll avoid self-limiting statements like, "I can't do that," or "He'll never like me."

Elizabeth wanted Craig to like her. They went out a couple of times and he tried to feel her breasts. She said she wasn't ready to do "sex things" with him, but all her friends were already doing them, so she admitted feeling pressure to conform. But she also didn't want Craig to lose interest in her, so she was torn about how to handle the situation. If she had a high CQ, she would tell herself it would be *she*--not Craig--who would decide when *she* was ready.

Instead, Elizabeth ended up telling herself, "I can't say 'no' to him. He'll dump me for another girl who will let him do these things." She continued to be his girlfriend, and gave in to "sex things" with him, even though she didn't feel ready.

If like Elizabeth you have ever been torn between what's right for you, boost your confidence now. Write the words "I can't say 'no'" on a piece of toilet paper, and flush it. Whenever you feel torn, write another self-limiting expression on more toilet paper, and flush that, too. Get in the habit of flushing away all the negative thoughts that keep you from making powerful decisions. Then sign the "10-Step CQ Booster Contract."

10-Step CQ Booster Contract

1. I will give myself a full hour of pleasure with anything that makes me feel great.

2. I will buy that new album I've been dying to get, and I'll play it a million times.

3. In my journal, I'll write 2 positive things each day, no matter how awful the day seemed.

4. I'll stand naked in the mirror and say 3 admiring things about my beautiful image.

5. This week, I'll return to my favorite activity that I somehow dropped.

6. I will round up my friends for 2 hours of laughter.

7. I will do something BOLD each day.

8. I will do a good deed, like volunteering in a hospital, working in a soup kitchen, or collecting   money for a charity.

9. I will dump the so-called "friends" who drain me.

10. I will study a role model who shows confidence, and I'll try to learn her secrets.

I agree to keep this promise with myself.

Signed:_____

   When you have a high CQ, you will exercise your voice about what is right for you. Sometimes you may even have to raise that voice!

Dear Dr. Gilda,

My boyfriend wants to have sex with me. He thinks sex would be a way for us to be closer. His friends have done it and they say it's great, and he wants to be like them. I already told him "no," and he knows I'm not backing down.

I believe he loves me and he's not using me. Besides, he respects my decision and he says it's not physical love we have. But he talks about having sex, as if this was a life or death situation . . . and that scares me!

I want to find other ways for us to feel closer as a couple. Besides, we are young and not ready for sex. I've told him how I feel, but his father told him that having sex was the best way for him to hold onto me. He said a counselor at his school said the same thing. I want him to know I'm not going anywhere, so he doesn't have to hold onto me like that!!

Please help me as quickly as you can. I know you're busy.
Fifie

Dear Fifie,

Good for you for knowing how you feel and sticking to your guns. Any guy who loves you will respect your wishes without pressuring you to give in to his. I find it hard to believe this guy's father and a school counselor told him that sex was the way he should hold onto you. Where would these adults be if you became pregnant or if you contracted a sexually transmitted disease?

Although you admit you're not emotionally ready for sex, you're certainly mature enough to speak your mind. Yay for you!! This guy may love you in his own way, but his pressure on you is selfish. Do you want to spend the next years of your life with a guy who's interested only in satisfying his desires?

If your boyfriend doesn't stop pressuring you, you'd better find another guy who hears you. You deserve to be respected and cherished.
Dr. Gilda

A girl who knows what is right for her, no matter what anyone else says, is a girl with a high CQ.

Step #3
ACHIEVE

Signing the above contract will put you on the road to achieving a strong CQ. Remember how amazed the Little Prince was to see 5,000 roses that all looked like the rose he knew on his tiny planet? Remember how he had to learn that his rose was different from the others? As you begin to raise your CQ, understand that you are unique from all the different people around you. Take the next quiz and find out what your special qualities actually are.

What Makes Me Unique?

1. The most positive messages my parents gave me were:

2.   Three cool words that describe me are:

   a)

   b)

   c)

3. My greatest accomplishment is:

4. My best friend would say my best trait is:

5. In school, I'm most proud of:

ScoreCard

Ask friends to take this quiz, too. Compare your answers and see how theirs differ from yours. Fortunately, you're all special and unique in your own way.

Unlike the toilet paper you flushed, fasten this Gilda-Gram® to your mirror so you can see it everywhere you go. Always remember your magnificence.

Gilda-Gram®
To raise your CQ,
Believe, Conceive, Achieve.

Are you convinced about your own uniqueness yet? Let's narrow your special qualities down to specific traits.

On the next quiz, circle the words that describe you. Then give the list to a good friend to circle the words she or he feels apply to you. Compare the two lists to see if friends perceive you as you perceive yourself.

Positive Personality Traits Quiz

Active

Affectionate

Ambitious

Assertive

Attractive

Caring

Cheerful

Considerate

Creative

Dependable

Determined

Entertaining

Enthusiastic

Friendly

Gentle

Genuine

Good-natured

Helpful

Humorous

Happy

Independent

Intelligent

Likable

Organized

Outgoing

Self-confident

Sensitive

Serious

Sincere

Sympathetic

Trusting

Truthful

Warm

Other Traits:

<u>ScoreCard</u>

This quiz checks your personality traits as you see them, and also checks how you appear to a friend. Besides those you and your friend circled, were there other traits you thought should be included? If so, add them to your list, get feedback from your friends about those you've added, and begin to think of them often.

Acting Out Your Traits

Each day, select one favorite word circled on your list. Look in the mirror and strike a pose that expresses that word. For example, if you chose "entertaining," pose, walk, and look like an *entertaining* person. Enjoy each trait--as only you can. Without sharing what you're doing, act out that word all day. Keep a log of people's reactions. These are all positive words, and you'll be exploring different parts of your personality.

A Word of Caution

You're on your way to achieving your plan for a higher CQ. But there is one thing you need to know as you start to make changes. When you're on your way to becoming an It Girl, others will notice. The so-called "friends" who knew you when your CQ was lower will sense something different about you. They probably won't know what to make of the new you.

Just because they notice, however, don't expect everyone to be happy. Some may accuse you of being suddenly conceited. Of course, you know better.

You know that raising your CQ is not conceit; it's a gift you are giving yourself to make you feel good and perform successfully. The bonus is you'll attract more *worthy* girlfriends and guys.

Some friends may try to get you to change back to the original you *they* were comfortable with. (Who's being selfish now?) Remember that your friends' judgments are not your problem.

Gilda-Gram®
**You are only responsible
for yourself and your own actions.**

Enjoy your new confidence, and the attention you're getting. You'll want to develop friendships with the people who are supportive. Moving toward new friends is a positive thing.

Outshouting Your Inner Critic

Despite all the work you've done to convince yourself you're terrific, sometimes parents, friends, siblings, or teachers can unknowingly say something negative that you can't easily forget. Some put-downs can become your negative "voice" or your self-doubting inner critic. Sometimes, this voice could overpower the one with the high CQ.

Your critical voice might trigger a short episode of self-bashing. Self-bashing can occur when you least want it to, like when that cute guy finally asks you out. You may find yourself saying stupid things, or sounding like a jerk. If that happens, follow the "4-Step Plan to Silence Your Inner Critic."

4-Step Plan to Silence Your Inner Critic

1. Acknowledge what your inner critic is trying to do and be ready to talk back.

2. Say out loud each negative thought your inner critic is sending your way.

3. Immediately substitute positive words, instead of the negative ones.

4. Convert each positive thought into an exciting goal.

Alice desperately wanted John to notice her. Finally, he was walking her way. "Omigod," she thought. "What will I do?" She began to feel her inner critic taking over, knowing that was not a good thing. So this is what she told it:

1. Alice's Inner Critic: "Oh, oh. Here comes John. Oh no! I look sooo fat."

2. Alice Said Out Loud, "I look so fat."

3. Alice's Positive Statement: "No, I am NOT sooo fat; I just *feel* fat. I'm still the same clothes size I was yesterday. But I am 4 pounds over my usual weight, and I am determined to lose these pounds."

4. Alice's Final Voice: "Starting today, I'm cutting out the rich desserts. Right this minute, I'm gonna make an impression on John."

Improving Your Confidence
When You're Blue

It would be great to think that It Girls feel good about themselves all the time. But everyone without exception has down days. Like other girls, It Girls get zits, they occasionally feel fat (especially during their periods), and they sometimes argue with their best friends, parents, and guys.

But It Girls have enough internal security to make a bad situation into a better one. They'll apply their favorite face cream to their zits and laugh that the zits will eventually disappear when they are ready. They'll wear baggy clothes on down days and they won't make a big deal out of feeling puffy. They'll make the first move toward patching things up with those with whom they argued, without feeling stupid.

Girls with good internal confidence can handle the down times better than those who don't think well of themselves. That's because people with strong feelings of security remember they're worthy of good things, and they know momentary lows are a fact of life, which eventually pass. In addition, girls with a strong sense of security know what to do to change a bad situation.

Girls with internal confidence can make bad situations improve quickly. It Girls are secure girls. They know they've got girl power, and they take charge. They're in control of themselves, without trying to control others.

Guys enjoy hunting for adventure. Because It Girls enjoy who they are even when guys are not around, they do their own thing and have fun. If and when a guy returns, an It Girl is that much more confident to deal with him *on her terms*.

NEED #2

Know How Guys Think

Girls who understand how guys think and function enjoy better relationships with them. Males and females are quite different, with different bodies, hormones, and brain structures--all of which cause differences in behavior. This is not to say that one gender is better than the other. It's just that we are *different*.

Studies show that girls get better grades, are more verbal, and are more likely to attend college, while boys demonstrate poorer reading and writing skills. The rash of school killings committed by boys has uncovered hidden low self-esteem of boys. Boys are more active than girls, and the school structure that demands obedience can create frustrated and aggressive young men.

There are ten million male teenagers in America. Any girl who wants to succeed with just one of them needs to understand where he's coming from.

Dr. Stephen Hinshaw, in his book, "The Triple Bind," explains the differences in the way girls and boys are groomed in childhood. Boys are trained to be assertive, self-confident, expressive, and committed to their agenda, and they don't apologize for these traits. In contrast, girls are also told to be ambitious, smart, and successful, but they get mixed messages that make it almost "impossible" to achieve them. For example: Be confident, but not conceited; Be smart, but not a know-it-all; Be ambitious and assertive, but don't upset anyone. As a result of these messages, women are more concerned than men for the way their behavior affects others. In my book, "Don't Bet on the Prince!" I give examples of the "Like Me" Language that females use where they aim for being "liked" over being "respected."

Unlike women, just as a car needs gas to run, guys are juiced by testosterone. Human males produce 7 to 10 times more testosterone than females. Testosterone pushes guys to grow taller, develop muscles, be more aggressive, compete, and want sex. Online, a guy by the name of Joshua says, "Guys talk about getting laid as often as possible. We're supposed to be getting it whenever and wherever we can. The talk is completely different for girls--only "sluts" give it up."

In contrast to guys' testosterone, girls have estrogen and progesterone, which cause them to develop into women, get pregnant, give birth, and bond with their babies and their man. Because girls menstruate, we are more aware of the mood swings females naturally experience. Periods and PMS act as a sort of monthly reminder of the changes female bodies undergo. Boys don't have those same triggers, and girls often don't realize males go through many body changes, too.

Hormones are substances in certain parts of the body that enter the blood stream and often influence behavior. They often flood the bodies of teens more quickly than their minds can handle. The rush of some hormones can cause teens to feel like fully-grown adults at times, yet moments later switch back to feeling like kids. When they occur, these changes can be frightening and confusing. They can result in rapidly fluctuating mood swings that cause teens to feel like strangers even to themselves.

Remember when you first got your period? Remember how irregular it was, with some skipped months, some months with heavy bleeding, and some months so light you hardly noticed you had it? Some girls take years before they become "regular," and some never have regularly predictable periods. Although guys don't bleed, they have hormonal swings just like you, and their emotions can seesaw from one extreme to another.

After knowing Ray for a few years as a friend, when they began to date, Joanie noticed his emotions flip-flopped. She complained, "He's on my volleyball team, which at first I thought was pretty cool. But now he's ruining it for me. He yells at people when they miss a pass, and he's really rude to everyone in the game. Then, when we have bio together he's a totally different person. He's an asshole in gym, then a Romeo when we're in class together."

She continued, "Guys transform into complete idiots when they're involved in sports. I've noticed there's not one guy I know who's normal when he's playing sports. They get into an ego trip, and show a totally different side of themselves. You say, 'Wait, I liked *him*?' But then out of the blue, he does something so sweet, and you think that you're the crazy one!"

Joanie's right. The interests, moods, and attention spans of Ray and his friends change at the drop of a hat. This fickleness is part of being a teen boy. To play to their short attentions, one wise TV network with a young male audience was planning 15-minute shows, instead of the usual 30 minutes.

Dear Dr. Gilda,

I need help. My boyfriend (who I really love) sometimes acts a little weird. One day, he says he loves me, and the next day, I try to sit by him, and he yells at my friend, and tells her to make me sit somewhere else. I don't understand him! Now his friends have been telling me things about him liking someone else. I trust him and my friends, and they tell me he isn't. I'm being driven crazy. Please help!!
Karen

Here are the reasons behind the flip-flopped behaviors of boys. Guys get 5 to 7 surges of testosterone a day, with an average of 11 erections. Five of those 11 occur while they're sleeping. These testosterone surges stimulate a boy's desire to masturbate a lot and to think about sex. The testosterone surges also make these guys act aggressively and competitively in sports, have fights, do dangerous things, or just show off.

It may seem like girls are the only ones

concerned about their body and their looks. But boys, too, worry about their image and shape. The muscular male action figures of dolls like GI Joe promote the same unrealistic expectations in guys that girls have suffered with their Barbies. Along with the eating disorders guys now have, they also crave huge biceps and an extreme desire for competition and control.

Anyone would think the testosterone urges are driven by the sex glands. But actually, their source is the three-pound blob of gray and white matter known as the brain. Researchers once believed brain development was complete by puberty. But the part of the brain that controls emotions and good judgment is not fully mature until the age of 25.

Brains are divided into the left and right hemispheres, joined by a cluster of nerves called the corpus callosum. The left side of the brain controls analytical thought and precise language--at which many boys excel. The right side of the brain is responsible for creativity and intuition, which many girls display.

Boys' brains are about 10 percent larger than girls' brains, but the corpus callosum is thicker in the brains of girls, making it easier for them to quickly switch back and forth between left-brain and right- brain activities. So, girls can brainstorm about relationships on the phone with friends (a right brain function), and *at the same time* solve complex math homework problems (a left-brain function).

In contrast, because of their thin corpus callosum, guys find it easier to perform activities on one side of the brain at a time, completing one activity before tackling another.

Also, because of the way their brains are wired, girls use more vocabulary words than boys, they speak more freely about feelings, and they use more variety in their language. It's a wonder our two sexes can communicate at all!

If a guy makes a girl angry, she may cut him down with her words, and probably leave him dumbfounded, since he doesn't have such a fine ability with words to retaliate. In contrast, when a guy becomes angry, he's more prepared to react in a loud and violent way.

The differences between the way little boys and little girls are raised are startling. In studies observing children playing in the sandbox, it has been documented that different discipline approaches from parents are encouraged for each gender.

For example, if a little girl throws sand at a playmate, her mother scolds her to "play nice." But if her brother acts in a similarly aggressive way, his mother is more accepting of his behavior, and may ignore it. As a college professor, I discussed these differences with a group of my students.

A young father didn't believe me. He said he had both a little girl and a little boy, three and four years old, respectively. He insisted that his wife would never show such obvious favoritism. I encouraged him not to believe me, but to observe his kids' actions, along with those of his wife and himself the next time he watched them play.

In our next class meeting, my student apologized. He said he honestly couldn't imagine a parent could raise two children so differently. He said he actually saw his wife *permitting* and *encouraging* his son's aggressive behaviors, while she came down hard on his daughter when she tried to do the same!

There are many more differences in the way girls and boys are raised. Girls are allowed to cry as an outlet for feeling sad and depressed. Boys are told to "be a man," which means, "It's not okay to cry, but it is all right to demonstrate anger." Actually, boys are not encouraged to even admit they feel depressed; that's a girl's thing. As a result, girls at 18 are twice as likely to admit they're depressed as boys the same age.

University of Michigan and Princeton University researchers asked adolescents what they worried about. Girls said looks, friends, family, self-worth, and safety, while boys said *performing* well in sports. When profiles were written about the perpetrators of the most violent school acts, it was discovered that each of the boys had been teased by classmates or rejected by girlfriends. Without an acceptable outlet for letting off steam--except through anger--these boys were unable to contain their feelings of being cut down.

If boys don't feel comfortable communicating their feelings, their anger has nowhere to go but to blow up in violence. True to their caveman ancestors, despite anti-gun lobbyists, boys are still encouraged to be hunters who use weapons.

I appeared on Court TV to comment on a murder trial of a man with a stepson. It was revealed that the five-year-old boy often greeted his stepdad by pulling out his fake gun, aiming it at the man, and imitating a gun battle in the Wild West. In response, his stepfather would remove his own *real* gun, aim it at the child, and do the same thing. In this family's *culture,* this was how the two males demonstrated love!

There are additional differences between the sexes. Directed from the right side of the brain, guys excel at spatial tasks or activities that require the use of space, like building things, fixing cars, or playing ball. This is an important fact stemming back millions of years to when males went out to find food, and females stayed in the cave to raise the kids. Men were hunters, and hunting is a spatial task.

When an animal moved through space, the caveman had to be successful in killing it to provide food for his family. To be equipped to survive the difficulties of the hunt and the outdoors, men developed thick muscles and less body fat than women to use their aggressions and competitive instincts to outsmart the animals. They had no need to discuss their deep feelings, or to speak about love and commitment.

We may be years beyond that now, but today's male behaviors have not changed much from those of millions of years ago. Men still hunt (even for action and adventure), and they'd rather perform spatial activities than talk about feelings and relationships, which women enjoy. For every one word a 12-year-old boy uses, a 12-year-old girl will use three to five. This lack of conversation frustrates the girls involved with these guys.

An It Girl understands what motivates male behavior. She can laugh at guys acting out, as long as they're not acting out against her. She accepts their aggressiveness as a form of "physical communication," since they're less able at verbal communication. Of course, a wise girl will surely leave a guy whose actions are violent.

A wise girl also won't jump into bed with a guy just because he pressures her. The University of Florida found that three out of four males would say "yes" to sleeping with a strange woman. In contrast, 100% of the females studied not only refused, but were also offended by the horny guy's offer. So males and females react differently to the opportunity for casual sex.

Dear Dr. Gilda,
I'm seeing a girl I'm intimate with. But I'm not really "into" the relationship. It's not that I don't like her; it's that she's just okay. Now this other girl wants to date me. I really like her. So I'm not sure how to handle it. I told the girl I'm seeing not to get attached to me. But she did.

Am I making a mistake by 1) wanting to date this other girl, and 2) seeing someone I can't put my heart into? Please, please help me!
Neil

Dear Neil,

I receive lots of emails from girls who get hurt because their guy either ends up cheating on them openly, or sneaks behind their backs with other girls. You obviously are sensitive enough to write to me about being conflicted. Good for you!

A lot of guys would simply do what their hormones dictate. But you know that your "girlfriend" has feelings for you and will be hurt if you cheat.

Even though you told her not to get attached to you, she did. It's not fair to continue leading her on. Sure, it's free sex for you, without strings. But you're setting her up for pain.

The fairest thing is to break it off and let her go. This will allow you to be free to date anyone you like, to not feel constricted by a girlfriend, and to explore a relationship with someone you care about.

Understand that many girls believe that no matter what a guy tells them, if he's having sex with them, he cares. You know better. So be a cool guy and let this girl go. She'll be upset at first, but it's the right thing to do.

On behalf of the entire female population, I thank you for your sincerity.
Dr. Gilda

It Girls acknowledge they have much at stake, and therefore take a cautious approach to having sex with a guy. Females who are choosier about who they want as a boyfriend cause males to work hard to get their attention.

Guys may say, "I love you" when they don't mean it, and they may make empty promises to get what they want. It Girls are aware these guys are thinking with the wrong body parts. Girls who want sincere guys won't bed down a guy they hardly know.

I appeared on TV's popular NBC Dateline to discuss the pros and cons of coed sleepovers for teens. Especially where kids are drinking and the hours are getting late, parents would rather have groups of teens sleep in the basement of one of their homes, than allow them to drive intoxicated.

On the surface, coed sleepovers seem like a safer choice. Dateline interviewed some very responsible-seeming high school kids and their parents who said their coed sleepovers were safe, fun events, and no drinking or sex occurred because all the kids were friends.

I vehemently upheld the unpopular position that even if the kids were friends, teen boys' hormones notoriously spike. This puts these teens at the disadvantage of a) perhaps having to deal with their sexual urges in mixed company, and b) perhaps having to say "no" to the pressure of a "friendly" come-on.

Teens have enough stress. Why set them up for pressure when it can be avoided? Of course, even if these young people have the greatest intentions, the truth is that boys start producing sperm at 12½ years old, they have at least a few erections while asleep (not to mention those they have while awake), and the number of sperm cells in an average ejaculation is 100 million. Adults complain about the problems of casual sex, STDs, and teen pregnancy. Why make those possibilities so easily available?

How to Trust Your Guy

A problem with teen testosterone arises when a girl thinks she can count on a guy she likes, and she finds out otherwise. A girl wants to believe a guy's promises that he cares for her and will have her back when she needs him.

With testosterone surges, a once-dependable guy suddenly becomes some aggressive freak that his girlfriend doesn't recognize. The girl feels abandoned and her trust disappears. If this happens often enough, a teen girl's trust in all guys erodes, and I receive emails like these:

Dear Dr. Gilda,
I have been dating my boyfriend for over 3 years. I love him, but I can't trust him. He hasn't done anything for me not to trust him. But it's happened to me before. How do I learn to trust him before it's too late?
Marie

Dear Marie,
Your boyfriend is suffering the consequences of *your* past. Think of the guy who hurt you earlier and realize he is not your boyfriend. Accept your boyfriend

for the wonderful person he is. Remind yourself of his positive qualities and the reasons you connected with him three years ago.

If you continue to concentrate on distrustful things you expect him to do, you are not being fair to him or to the relationship. Trust must begin somewhere—and it's got to start with you.
Dr. Gilda

When a girl accuses a guy of doing deeds he didn't do, she's in jeopardy of losing him. This is happening to Concerned after only two months.

Dear Dr. Gilda,
I've been dating this great guy for two months. When I'm not around him or don't know what he's doing, I get nervous thinking he's cheating, even though he probably isn't. He gets mad when I accuse him. I try to trust, but it's hard. How do I trust him when we're not together?
Concerned

Dear Concerned,
You are right to recognize this is a problem. Guys don't like being accused of cheating when they aren't. If you put cheating ideas in your boyfriend's head, who knows what weird way he'll react? Guys have told me, "She thinks I'm cheating and she constantly nags me about it. So I might as well cheat. She thinks I'm doing it anyway." Don't let this happen to you.

Your distrust is coming from your feelings of

insecurity. It's only been two months and you're still getting to know each other. If he's a cool guy, over time he will give you reason to feel more secure.

Have a heart-to-heart with your guy and share your feelings. Tell him you would feel more secure if he could call you more often to prove he cares.

Of course, he may feel controlled by your request to "check in" with you. Some guys actually want their girlfriends to think they're desirable to other girls, so they go out of their way to make them jealous. That's immature, and you don't need that kind of guy.
Dr. Gilda

Sometimes, testosterone surges cause guys to stupidly show off. But while they're in the "high" of their show-off moment, they may embarrass their girlfriend. If a guy continues to embarrass her, she will lose trust in him. Once trust is lost, it is hard to get back.

Dear Dr. Gilda,
I love my boyfriend to death, but he did something that made me lose my trust in him. It's been a while, and I want to know how I can get that trust back. I think this is the guy I want to marry someday. Help!
Heather

Dear Heather,
Tell your guy how you feel. He will need to prove you can trust him again. This is the consequence of stupid past actions. Whatever you do, don't even

think of marrying him until this trust issue is resolved. A marriage based on *dis*trust can't survive.

If you don't resolve this issue now, your negative feelings toward your guy will worsen as he continues to disappoint you. You don't need a divorce before you get a marriage!
Dr. Gilda

As you can see from my responses, communicating honestly with your boyfriend is key to keeping love alive. If you feel your guy is not receptive to your openness or he's not sensitive to your special feelings, it's best you discover that now.

There are usually good reasons for a girl not trusting a guy. Some of these reasons are serious.

Dear Dr. Gilda,
    I have a little problem. I'm 16 years old and living in a small town in Texas. I have been talking to this guy for some time, and I feel I'm getting closer to him every day. At first, when we started talking I really didn't want to get close to him because of my past. I was raped when I was 14 and I had a few boyfriends who hit me. So when I started talking to Juan I wanted to take everything slow.

Although we have known each other a year, we've been talking seriously for 6 months. We were always good friends. Juan had always wanted a relationship with me, but I never gave him the time of day.

Now I know how to be in a relationship, but I'm

scared I won't be able to trust him. I told him that is the only reason I can't go out with him. I can't even trust my own father and brother, although they have never done anything to me. It's just that I don't trust any man.

Should I be able to trust Juan now (considering he has never done anything to hurt me and I feel I am in love), or should I just call it off? Shouldn't I be able to forget my past? Or should I hide from men for the rest of my life?
Michelle

Dear Michelle,
With all you've been through, of course trust is an issue for you.

Gilda-Gram®
25% of all teen girls
experience dating violence.

The majority of dating violence incidents occur when a relationship is a serious, steady one! It's a horrible thought that girls who are out with guys they know and trust end up being violated. But to think the only way around this is to "hide" for the rest of your life is unfair to you.

Before you do another thing, find a female counselor who specializes in rape issues. You will also want to understand why you attracted guys who hit you. You have a whole life ahead.

If you don't handle your past, you'll be denying yourself and Juan the opportunity of seeing what can

happen. Even if this relationship doesn't work out, learn how to put your history behind you. Counseling will help you enjoy a glorious future.
Dr. Gilda

Trust takes time. Two people must get to know each other, see each other when things are good, but also experience the bad times. Girls should observe their boyfriend being sad, upset, and angry, and they should note how he deals with situations that don't go his way.

Even when you think you really know someone, sometimes you're shocked by a new, "strange" antic.

Dear Dr. Gilda,
I am from West Virginia, and I need your help really bad!!! I have this boyfriend who I've dated for two years. Lately, we have been arguing over stupid things, like me talking to one of his "ex-friends," as he calls him.

The other day, he threw a chair and broke it when he got mad at me. A week later, he hit the bathroom door and put a hole in it about an inch from my head. He said he was mad at me again. I thought I loved him, but now I'm not sure. What do I do?
Candy

Dear Candy,
You thought you knew this guy well, and now he's blowing his cork each time he is frustrated with something you do. He must get help at once. Until he does, steer clear of him. So far, he's only done harm to objects. When tempers flare, a person can totally lose

control to the point of hurting people around him.

Perhaps he needs to be on medication, or maybe he needs anger management classes. He must speak to a therapist to determine the cause of his outbursts. But whatever he does, you must protect yourself.

Tell him you're freeing yourself of him until he takes care of his problem. If he tells you he doesn't have a problem, stay away indefinitely.
Dr. Gilda

It takes a while until someone is comfortable enough to reveal his true personality. So I advise young women not to jump into steady relationships too soon.

Gilda-Gram®
Trust begins by trusting
your own judgment.

Young women can usually tell when a guy's only interested in a fling. Even if they choose to ignore the obvious signs, they know when someone is not good for them.

Dear Dr. Gilda,
My boyfriend asked me out because he and his friends made a bet they have to ask someone out. I'm not sure if he really likes me because he rarely calls and he flirts with my friends.
Brittany

Dear Brittany,
Girl, you don't need me to tell you what you already know. This guy is flirting with other girls and is

more devoted to his pals than to you. Find someone who genuinely wants to be with you!
Dr. Gilda

Brittany's dilemma is obvious. Of course, it's much too early for her to even be calling him her "boyfriend."

But what if she's one of those girls who refuses to heed the blaring signs this guy will turn into a heartbreaker? What if she continues to crush on this "boyfriend," and will not stop until the signals hit her over the head? Here are some signs that help girls wise up.

Signs Your Guy's a Two-Timer

If you even *suspect* your guy is wandering, read these more obvious signs:

1. He *suddenly* douses himself with so much cologne he can attract insects. He has added new jewelry, a different look, or a new haircut.

2. He *suddenly* alters his usual behavior, either presenting you with lots of gifts and affection when he's never behaved this way or stopping the usual nice things he has been doing for you.

3. His technology habits are *suddenly* different. His phone rings with unfamiliar numbers or he doesn't answer his phone when you're

around.

4. He breaks dates, offering lame excuses that don't add up.

If these sound familiar, get wise! A girl doesn't need to be with a jerk who doesn't appreciate her. If he'd rather get his ego massaged by other skirts, pack him in.

I received a disturbing email from a testosterone-crazed guy who admitted he needed my help.

Hey Doc,

I don't know why I do this to myself, but I'm falling for this girl, Mary. She's the girl I've been waiting for my whole life. She is 18, 5'11", 150 pounds, very sweet and innocent (she's still a virgin!), and gorgeous. She played basketball in high school, but doesn't love the game anymore. She runs every morning, and the only bad thing is that she has a boyfriend. I don't know what to do.

The past few nights I have been up in her dorm room hanging out and talking. She told me that I'm special, I'm a really great guy, and whoever I'm with is a lucky girl. (I didn't tell her about Jenni, my girlfriend back home, but she knows about the girl I'm sleeping with in college, Valori.) She is just so damn adorable. She calls me Richard (instead of Rick), and I have a nickname for her and she said I'm the only one allowed to use it. It's "Cheeks" because she has the most adorable cheeks when she smiles. They come up, I pinch them, and she giggles.

Man, I don't know what to do. Should I distance myself from her to let my feelings cool down? Should I pursue her? Or should I just chill? What, what, what?
Thick Rick

Dear Thick Rick,
WHAT, indeed!! You have a girl back home (waiting patiently for you), you have one you're sleeping with in college—who you tell the girl back home about, and now you want to have "the girl of your dreams" who you've waited for your "whole life."

Buddy, you're not being fair to any of these women. But frankly, if they're stupid enough to go for your lines and cheating ways, they deserve you.

If you have any decency, you'll leave Mary alone. Forget about trespassing on another's guy's territory. Besides, you'd probably get bored with her if she were to become yours. Grow up!
Dr. Gilda

Self-involved Thick Rick really *is* thick! He worries his confusion is driving him crazy. Little does he care about the girls he's hurting.

You've learned the traits that make a guy cool. Now assess the guys you know that you might never have thought of as boyfriend material. The more you rate different personalities accurately, the more you should compliment yourself on your ability to trust your heart.

Gilda-Gram®
Trust your guy-ger counter to show you how to keep the best and dump the rest.

So what's a good girl to do about the natural impulses that flood the body of a guy? Surely, she can't help what's going on inside him, nor is she responsible for his aggression. Unless his behavior threatens her safety or reputation, it's not her concern.

Gilda-Gram®
Get to REALLY know a guy, before you have sex with him.

A guy's testosterone surges will continue to overwhelm him. Just be sure they don't also overwhelm you.

Testosterone Tester

1. Does he think he's Hercules and can take on the world?

2. Does he believe he's better than everyone else?

3. Does he think it's okay to flirt with other girls in front of you?

ScoreCard

If you answer "yes" to any of these, reconsider how "great" your guy *really* is.

Dear Dr. Gilda,

My boyfriend is usually wonderful towards me, but out of blue he'll start flirting with other girls in front of me, as though I'm not there. We get into fights as a result. What can I do?

He knows this is destroying me. I've tried not to get mad, but it's so hard seeing this right before my eyes. It seems he doesn't care if he makes me mad. Later he'll act like nothing happened. How can I look past his behavior and try to change my feelings? I don't want to let him go. He means too much to me.
Audrey

Dear Audrey,

Your boyfriend's testosterone surges might explain his sudden changes. However, just because you understand his behavior doesn't mean you must put up with being dissed. What disturbed me most about your email is your question about how to "look past his behavior and try to change your feelings."

You have a right to your feelings and you never want to change them. They are an alarm that tells you you're not being respected, and to communicate with your guy about his poor treatment of you.

After you confront your guy he may not understand what you're talking about. If he chooses not to curb his aggressions, he's letting you know how little you mean to him.

You're right in saying he means *too much* to you. Nobody should mean so much to someone that she

disregards her own feelings. If this guy will not adore you, find someone who will.
Dr. Gilda

While guys have their testosterone surges, girls experience their own hormonal changes. If each time a girl menstruates, her guy says, "The bitch is back," he won't hang around long, will he? And why should he? There is never any excuse to be disrespectful to people we supposedly care for.

While we can benefit from the information that tells us why guys act the way they do, it does not give them license to mistreat girls. This goes for both sexes.

If you are being dissed by the guy who has pledged to love you, examine how you feel about this. Confront him in a calm and open way, but if he refuses to curb his outbursts, take care of yourself by leaving. Whether you return can be determined after you've both had a break.

In the meantime, if your dude's moods continue to be an issue, do a mood check on him to determine whether you want to keep him.

Check the Mood of Your Dude

Does your guy have a steady personality, or do his moods swing from one extreme to another? Write Yes or No beside each of question below.

_____1. Does he believe he's better than other people?

_____2. Does he flaunt his money, clothes, or car?

_____3. Does he brag about scoring with girls?

_____4. Is he insensitive to animals and children?

_____5. Does he flirt with girls in front of you?

_____6. Does he treat waiters and other service workers poorly?

ScoreCard

<u>1 - 2 Yeses</u>: Remind him why you like him, and explain it's not for his showy strutting.

<u>2 - 4 Yeses</u>: Express your disappointment in his behavior because he's not showing the qualities about him you like best.

<u>5 - 6 Yeses</u>: Don't waste your time trying to reason with him. He's a testosterone junkie, with mucho macho. Although you may want to tell him why you're packing him in, your best bet is to get out ASAP.

When a girl likes a guy, she should be sure he _enhances_ her. When his testosterone surges try to dominate her, an It Girl will stand her ground. But she also knows she's not his mother or teacher.

Gilda-Gram®
**Girls don't have to educate guys.
They just have to reject their nonsense.**

If a girl's not strong before she enters into coupledom, she will continually be disappointed.

<u>What I Do For Love</u>

Guys may seem hard headed when it comes to romance, but they aren't dumb. Many of them need coaxing to find words of caring. And although they might get teased by their buddies, most of them want to feel close to someone.

Do you think guys have easier lives than girls? Complete the following sentence:

"If I woke up as a boy,

_____."

Some young women answered:

1. I'd pee standing up.

2. I'd take off my shirt and swim.

3. I'd walk around in just boxers.

4. I'd do my hair without gel.

5. I'd scratch my balls.

6. I'd lose my bra.

While these responses might not seem earth shattering, they show the effort girls put into the daily course of being feminine. Even if they already have a boyfriend, they constantly feel the pressure to impress.

One girl in a relationship for three months revealed, "If I'm in a bad mood, I'll scream, yell, and curse with my girlfriends, but when I'm around Carl, I refrain from acting upset." As soon as guys enter the picture, many girls take on a new identity!!

Too many girls are boy pleasers. They cook and bake for him, they over-apologize, they always make themselves available, they inconvenience themselves to please him, they have trouble telling him "no," and they put their own needs and goals on hold.

Especially upsetting was a news article about 13- and 14-year-old girls in a Virginia middle school who were giving guys oral sex. The girls named the act "a popularity kind of thing," and agreed that such hooking up could last a few weeks or a few hours.

Unfortunately, while the guys asked the girls to perform this act on them, the girls wanted full-blown relationships, which they didn't get. So the boys received sexual gratification but the girls felt demeaned. Why are girls so willing to do anything to win guys' love?

Fitting in is one of the greatest challenges young women have. In one study, the "cool" crowd is often defined by money. Money buys the best clothes, technology, and cars, and for many, you're just invisible unless you sport the right brands.

At first, a girl may feel delighted to be let into

the cool crowd. But after a while, blind belonging begins to take its toll. It's dangerous to enact behavior that makes you feel uncomfortable. Resisting peer pressure may be tough, but if you lose your values, life can become a lot tougher.

Gilda-Gram®
Don't put out
to fit in!

A girl who prostitutes her body puts herself down. Susan went to a party and met Bernard. They hooked up immediately. As soon as they kissed, Susan thought Bernard was a bad kisser. But she rationalized, "He's really nice and he likes me. So I'll stay with him tonight because I feel obligated."

What?? Susan stayed with Bernard at the party the entire night, and maybe missed out on meeting someone she liked better. She said she didn't want him to feel she was just using him. She feared he'd call her a "bitch" if she just kissed him and left.

I said, "Where is your obligation to yourself?"

Susan didn't know. If she had been an It Girl, she would have known she must honor herself as Number One.

Sometimes, the stories I hear go a lot further than just kissing.

Dear Dr. Gilda,
I'm 14 and pregnant with my ex's baby. After we had sex, everything changed. He acted different toward

me. Before that, he was sweet and seemed to care. Now I don't know what to do. Please help!
Therese

Dear Therese,
It's too late for me to tell you the sad statistic that ninety percent of the males who impregnate a teen girl abandon her and her family. Find an adult you can trust, and discuss your next plans with that person.
Dr. Gilda

Therese discovered that having a guy is not as important as it had seemed.

Gilda-Gram®
**Finding a boyfriend is not
a gotta-get-it goal.**

When a girl becomes so boy-crazy that she puts a guy on a pedestal, she gives away everything. Not treating yourself like Number One only brings you disrespect. And disrespect can make a girl feel worse than she felt when she was without a guy!

He May Be Aggressive, But He Still Wants Love

If you don't believe that guys want love as much as girls do, read the emails I received from guys 14 to 25. Guys want caring, although they may not seem compassionate in their attempts to get it.

Dear Dr. Gilda,

This may sound weird, but how do I get a girl to like me?

Luke

Dear Dr. Gilda,

There's a friend I have known for about 3 years who I really love. She doesn't know how I feel. I have tried to tell her a few times, but every time I try I chicken out. Any suggestions?

Tortured

Dear Dr. Gilda,

My girlfriend and I have been broken up for about a week now, and I still love her so much! Since Valentine's Day is coming up, what should I give her, so she would know I love her?

H.H.

Dear Dr. Gilda,

Well, I just asked out this girl who I liked for a long time. I had given her a rose, and it was really sweet, but that is the trouble. I want to be the sweetest and best man she has ever known. I'm 22, and I'm not sure what things I should do.

Tim

Dear Dr. Gilda,

I've never been in love before. I recently met someone perfect for me. The thing is, she doesn't want to get serious with anyone because her last relationships ended badly.

I've made my feelings clear to her. We've only

been out a few times, so maybe it's too early for her to decide. How can I convince her, without rushing or pressuring her?
Bob

Dear Dr. Gilda,

I am wondering if you can tell me what is most likely going on in my ex-girlfriend's head to hurt me the way she has. We've been together for 3 years, when she was not even 14 and I was 16. We became really close quickly and had been great friends for these past few years. But things suddenly changed.

My brother started bringing around a friend who took a liking to my girlfriend. We would all hang out together, drinking every night when I noticed all my girlfriend and that kid did was talk by themselves. They exchanged a lot of eye contact and smiles. They would follow each other to the bathroom and take longer than they should to return. This all went on in my own house.

I took this kid in as a friend and actually took him on vacation with us. My girl and I probably had twenty to thirty fights about him and she told me I was crazy for even suggesting they liked each other. Love-blind me believed her. Two months ago, we decided we needed space. Now she says her feelings have changed for me because I treated her badly.

I don't deny I did do some bad things, but I promised her I would change. She tells me she needs time to straighten her head out, and I should stop begging her to come back because she is looking at me as a weak person she could never be with. She tells me she needs time to miss me.

Will she ever wake up? She's the one who begged me to put a ring on her finger. What is she doing now? She has torn my world upside down.
Broken Up Les

Dear Dr. Gilda,

I've been really good friends with this girl for a year. We have always been attracted to each other, and she finally broke up with her boyfriend. We slept with each other about a week later and it totally changed our relationship, as I knew it would. She is now back with her man and I don't know what to do.

She is still attracted to me, and says she would break up with her man for me when I come back from college. (I am leaving for college for two years. She wants me to come back home and marry her!) There is a slight problem: age. She is 17 and I am 20. Please help!?!
Al

Boys want love as much as girls do, and their feelings are just as sensitive. They want to find answers to their love problems, but they don't know whom to ask. I receive a lot of email from boys because they can be anonymous and still keep their egos intact.

Without knowing how to behave, they often end up acting stupid and looking foolish. Or they act totally disinterested and aloof.

<u>Unacceptable Behavior from Guys</u>

No matter how sensitive a boy is or how stupidly he behaves, the only thing that counts is how he behaves toward YOU. Sometimes, you may have to get him alone for his real caring to show.

But if he's rude and disrespectful in front of others, no matter how much good you see in him when his friends aren't around, he's a loser. Tell him you will not accept this treatment. If he doesn't respect you, dump him!

Elaine learned early that Marc was not someone she could count on. Despite liking him, she felt ambivalent about wanting him as a boyfriend. The two of them were having one of their typical flirting sessions one day after school:

Marc: "So when are you gonna give me head?"

Elaine: Laughs, "Oh, Marc, stop it."

Marc: "Are you coming home on the bus?"

Elaine: "Yes."

Marc: "Good. We can get started right away."

Elaine enjoyed the attention, but she never considered that the way Marc spoke to her was disrespectful. When I raised the issue with her and said she should not allow boys to speak to her in dirty ways, she admitted she "sort of" knew that.

When I asked why she puts up with it, she answered, "Aside from his horniness, he's a good friend. He just sometimes thinks with his other head. He's so sweet when he's not horny. We talk. He gives me advice. He wants sex, but he doesn't want to go out with me."

Elaine wished Marc would ask her out to prove he liked her as more than a friend. Yet she came to recognize that was not Marc's intention. He enjoyed their friendship, but that was a separate issue for him. He wasn't looking for a steady girlfriend. He just wanted a girl to have sex with, like any testosterone-crazed boy. Wisely, Elaine vowed she'd never be that girl.

The fact that Elaine was willing to play along in the flirtation proved how she was willing to put her values on hold to get a boy's attention. "Sort of" knowing she was being disrespected, she still tried to laugh it off.

Unlike a lot of girls, Elaine was smart not to trick herself into believing Marc cared for her. However, she was also not confident enough to tell him to flake off.

In contrast, some girls invite punishment by still trying to win their crush's heart, no matter how rude he may be.

Dear Dr. Gilda,
     I went out with a guy last year for a few months

and we broke up. I have liked one of his friends for a long time, but all he does is call me rude names. I think it is because my ex-boyfriend tells him to say dirty things to me. How can I get him to like me as a friend or maybe more?
Helpless

Dear Helpless,
The name you use tells me a lot about you. "Helpless" makes you sound like you have no say in this game of mean. Realize this guy is a jerk if he's acting only on the advice of your ex-boyfriend. You need a guy who thinks for himself.

But even if he's thinking it's okay to say mean things to you, why would you want such a fool?

Observe how any respectful couple speaks to each other, and how the guy treats the girl. Tell yourself you deserve that kind of treatment.
Dr. Gilda

I receive a lot of emails from young women upset with the name-calling. Name-calling does hurt, especially if you accept the names are true.

Dear Dr. Gilda,
I just broke up with my baby's father and he says I can't get anyone else. I can't eat or sleep, and I don't want to go anywhere. What should I do?
Cara

Dear Cara,

Why do you believe the names your baby's father calls you? The moment you allow his words to destroy you, that's the moment you give him total control over your life. Release the spell he has over you, and tell yourself the positive things about how wonderful you really are!
Dr. Gilda

Since a guy's hormones often rule him, a girl must honor her own interests and rule herself. She must decide whether she's getting enough caring from the guy she's with. If the guy is benefitting from the relationship at the girl's expense, she must let him go.

Dear Dr. Gilda,
I am 17 years old, and I have a five-month-old baby girl by this guy I've been with for two years. He and I have had a very abusive relationship and he is always putting me down. He has hit me and put me down for the last time.

I finally called the cops. He is now on the run from them. He always calls and stops by not to see his daughter, but to have sex and be mean to me. I don't know why I continue letting him do this. I beg him to see his daughter, hold her, and play with her, but he doesn't. Then he says I am taking him away from his little girl.

I don't trust any man. Yet I still want him. What is wrong with me? Please help me get over him. He is driving me crazy. I think about him all the time. I can't eat, sleep, or be happy. I am a very good mom and I

work two jobs and go to school. What should I do to get my life back together? I saw you on TV and you are beautiful!! I know you can help me.
Cookie

Dear Cookie,
You have been allowing yourself to be taken in by this guy's "charms"—but he's not very charming. A guy who puts you down and hits you is out of control. When someone is out of control he uses his hands. That's not being a man. That's a scared animal that feels it must use force to get what it wants.

You're trying to make something of your life by improving yourself in school, work, and motherhood. But you're not being the best mother you can be if you allow your little girl to observe a woman being a punching bag for a guy.

You're bonded to this guy by your child. You've also spent two years of your life with him, with a lot of experiences. So of course you feel close to him. But he's toxic for both you and your daughter. Is this what you want your little girl to see? Is this how you want her to think all men treat women?

Tell yourself you deserve a man to love you in a positive way. Tell yourself you'll accept only the very best treatment. Tell yourself you'd rather be alone than be with an abuser. Never again be alone with this guy. When he visits the baby, have another adult present to insure your safety. Domestic violence usually occurs with people we know who profess their love for us. This is how a lot of women get murdered.

Your daughter needs you to be her role model so she doesn't eventually become one of those horrible statistics.

Dr. Gilda

Girls Can Be Aggressive, Too

Girls are becoming more aggressive, while guys are becoming more sensitive. This may be a good change because it takes some pressure off the guys to be in constant control. It may also motivate girls to be more independent and assertive in seeking and satisfying their goals.

Yet no matter what societal changes occur, girls' brains produce more serotonin than guys' brains. Serotonin is a brain chemical that inhibits aggressive behavior. So while girls may think it's all right to stand up to their men when they're being abused, they still feel uncomfortable when they do it.

The same happens when girls ask guys out. They have reservations about what might happen if the guy turns them down. Of course, nobody wants to be rejected.

Dear Dr. Gilda,

I like this guy and I think he might like me. I want to ask him out but I'm afraid of being rejected.

Smart, beautiful, and nice girls have asked him out, including my best friend, and he turned every one down. What do you think is his problem?
Real Interested

Dear Real Interested,
Maybe this guy is afraid of aggressive girls. If you really want to get close to a guy, establish a friendship with him first. Let him feel comfortable doing the asking.

Also recognize he may be into things other than dating. You can't make someone want you. If the timing is not right, there's nothing you can do. But you can try to interest him by being a real friend.
Dr. Gilda

Speaking of girls who allow their aggressions to run wild, I receive many notes from young women who think they have to act like men in combat.

Dear Dr. Gilda,
I had been seeing a guy for 3 months. I was at the movies with my friends when he and my male best friend were there.

Well, I saw him with a girl. He didn't know I was watching (actually snooping). The girl he was with kept looking at me. I said to my friend, "I'll be back." I walked up to her and told her if she didn't stop giggling and staring at me, I would deck her in the face. My man put his head down, and covered his face. I got kicked out of the movies because the girl tested me, and well, I hit her and she bled. I know that was wrong. I am sorry.

I have a current boyfriend, but sometimes I want to go back to my ex. I made the mistake of asking my ex out this morning and he said he'd get back to me. I have gotten myself into the biggest crap hole now. Can you give me ANY advice?

I have read all your articles and I see you on TV. I love your advice. I think my boyfriend really cares about me. But one reason I don't want to stay with him is because he wants to spend every waking moment with me and I don't want that! We know a lot about each other and we're real compatible. My ex and I are also compatible. My mom says changing my tastes is normal. Why is this happening?
Cassie

Dear Cassie,

Your mom's right that changing your tastes in guys is normal for young women. You're back and forth between these two guys because you haven't decided who you are and what you want. And it's also normal for you to want to flee from the guy who wants to own you 24/7. That's not a healthy relationship for either of you. You will probably be compatible with lots of guys before you settle down.

NEVER use physical force on anyone to prove your point. It was you who looked like a jerk when you hit that girl. Your ex was embarrassed by your outrageous behavior, and if you thought this was the way to win his heart, you were dead wrong. If your ex didn't want to be with this girl, he wouldn't have been there. And anyone can look at you and yes, even giggle, if they want to.

You know you were wrong and that is good. Work on your jealousy and indecision before you look for love.
Dr. Gilda

Some girls need encouragement to take the reins. Others take the reins and don't know what to do with them.

Dear Dr. Gilda,
There's this boy in my class, Shawn. He is hot and I want to date him. I am not sure if he likes me or how to tell him I like him. I've been playing footsy with him! What should I do next?
Toni

Dear Toni,
Take your free foot and use it to step on the one that's rubbing against Shawn. Get to know this guy before you push the physical on him. This way, if there's a chance he might be interested, he won't be frightened off.

Some guys fear that if a girl comes on strong at first, she'll try to control them later. A lot of guys will do anything to protect themselves from being controlled by a girl. Let the relationship unfold slowly if it's going to, and let Shawn think it was *he* who hunted *you* down!
Dr. Gilda

<u>When Girls' Aggressions Go Too Far</u>

Some girls don't know when to stop. At a wealthy New York private school, some sixth grade girls were found developing a private sign language to taunt their peers and cast "spells" on those they disliked. Teasing is mean-spirited by mean girls, and it hurts both the teaser and the teased.

Yet up to 94% of gang members, and 85% of juveniles in prison are male. So while girls' crimes have risen, their numbers don't compare with those of boys.

Girls feel comfortable being bolder than they were in the past. But testosterone is the main source of energy for boys. It's the reason they fly off the handle instead of cry. It's the reason they need to dominate their territory and sometimes their girlfriends. It's the reason they take up to seven hours longer than girls to process their feelings. It's the reason they try to fix crises as soon as they occur.

But like most people, boys want a challenge. For some guys, just the chase to try to score that hot chick is enough. Sometimes, when she finally declares her love they flee.

But the harder boys must work to win a girl's heart, the more they appreciate their prize. Although they may push her to give in to their desires, many boys lose respect the moment a girl says "yes."

Playing Hard to Get

To make themselves seem less available, a lot of girls are *taught* to play hard to get. They make themselves scarce when their guy is trying to find them, and they act like they have loads of guys drooling over them. I don't recommend girls play games in trying to get a guy to love them.

Gilda-Gram®
When we play games,
we attract game players.

Game players end up giving us back our own medicine. Would you be happy with a guy who purposely doesn't answer his phone or tries to make you jealous?

Gilda-Gram®
We attract the same behaviors in a guy
that we ourselves put forth.

Instead of *playing games*, young women should keep enjoying the activities they've always loved. If you're afraid you will lose him to someone else, recognize that nothing you do will keep him. A guy will stay with you *only* when he truly wants to!

Foolishly Putting Out for More

Linda was one of those girls who found out the hard way. She met Brad on Valentine's Day and really fell hard. She had sex with him the second time they met. Right after the act, he coldly said, "Linda, I really hope you didn't have sex with me thinking I'm gonna ask you out. I like you--but my mind is on Rachel. One day she's with her boyfriend, the next day she says she wants to be with me. I really like her and I hope our relationship can work."

Linda didn't even have the good sense to get out of there. Instead, she got it on with him again the same night, thinking she would change his mind. The next day, when they were online, they found they had nothing to talk about. Now, whenever they see each other, each detours in an opposite direction. Linda complains, "I can't believe Brad did that to me." I told her she *let* him!!

Guys are not that difficult to understand. They may appear otherwise, but they feel pressure to prove their manhood. They go out of their way to impress their buddies. They press girls for sex, burp, fart, act loud, and go out of their way to appear insensitive and hide their soft side. Yet despite all the show, they want love, just like girls. They just have a different way of showing it, fearing their pals will ridicule them.

It Girls know that boys' posturing is mucho macho stuff. Many times, girls must be detectives to find out what guys *really* mean by some of their bizarre antics. But girls must also be careful to protect their own values. While Linda gave her body and feelings to Brad, he was pining for Rachel who was giving him a hard time!

Unfortunately, Linda is not the only girl who lay on her back for a guy too soon.

Dear Dr. Gilda,

I have been going out with my boyfriend for two months. I've already had sex with him, but now it seems every time he comes over, we have to have sex. I want a real relationship, but all he wants is sex. What should I do?

Suffering

Dear Suffering,

You can never un-ring the bell. I wish I had received this email when you were merely *considering* having sex with him.

You rushed into things too quickly. Since you raised his level of expectation, he's expecting that level to continue indefinitely. Now you realize this is not what you want.

It's your precious body, and your needs are essential. If you don't want to have sex, honor yourself and refuse. If that means your boyfriend gets mad and leaves, let him go—with your blessing!

Dr. Gilda

Some girls just don't get it. Once a girl gives in to his pleading and begging, his challenge disappears because he's already won his prey and he may be ready to move on.

But when a girl has the strong inner self of an It Girl, she recognizes the surges her guy is experiencing have more to do with his hormones than the feelings of caring he claims to have for her. A girl with a strong inner self won't believe the "I love you's" that guys utter just to get a free feel or more.

Audrey's words that her boyfriend "means too much to me" place her at his command. No girl should devote her whole life counting on a guy to always be there for her. When she's independent, she will enjoy her own activities and friends.

Understanding guys is a big component of having successful relationships with them. Until you understand your guy, keep sex off the table.

Dear Dr. Gilda,
I'm 21, and my boyfriend and I will be going out for 3 months. I have really fallen hard for him. I know I love him, and he has been telling me he loves me, too.

We both want sex bad. But I'm scared he will tell everyone when we do have is, and I'll be labeled "easy," while he'll be called a "stud."

What should I do? He's already promised me he wouldn't tell anyone. But a guy's a guy, and I know they all tell people they had sex. Please help!
Melanie

Dear Melanie,
I'm glad you wrote to me before you did something you'd regret. Sex should be an expression of how two people feel towards each other. A guy who loves his girl will not brag at her expense. He'll respect her and her reputation by keeping their sex life private.

Obviously, you have reservations about trusting your guy. Try trusting him with a private secret, and see where he goes with that. It's better to be sure than sorry.
Dr. Gilda

Unlike a lot of girls who have sex and are sorry later, at least Melanie is thinking about the consequences of her actions before she acts. Check out what a guy is really feeling before you believe the words you want to hear.

Dear Dr. Gilda,
My boyfriend and I have been going out for 4 months. He says he loves me, but I haven't seen him for 3 weeks. He says it's because of his busy schedule. His parents are split up, so he has to make time for each of them. He is also in drama and runs track. Do you think he does really care, or do you think he's using his activities as an excuse not to see me so he can cheat behind my back?
Vicki

Dear Vicki,
Never be with a guy you can't trust. All the interests this guy has make him more interesting. But if he keeps saying he's "too busy" for you, find someone who's not.
Dr. Gilda

When two people understand each other, they can form a friendship based on respect, which can even expand to love. Respect is the basis for listening and communicating, but it takes time to unfold. Without respect, no relationship can survive.

Understanding where a guy is coming from is important because guys won't usually discuss their feelings. Make understanding a priority.

It's a rare guy who will want to just hang out and hug his girlfriend. The guy usually wants to complete his goal of having sex. But girls want to bond with a full relationship. So whom do you think will win this tug of war?

As a guy's frustration mounts, he may begin to pressure his girlfriend for sex. Many girls give in, not because they want sex but because they want to feel wanted, loved, and cherished. They want to be hugged, held, and told sweet words. They fear that if they say "no," he'll get it elsewhere and leave. If that happens to you, give him a Going Away party!

Having sex for fear you'll be dumped is no reason to put out. But some girls say they regret they didn't put out after their guy left for someone who would. That is crazy thinking!!

Dear Dr. Gilda,

I love your website. I'm 18 years old. Six months ago, I began dating a 24-year-old boy. Everything was going great. He showed me his love, I met his family, and I thought all was fine.

He always wants to be in bars and at parties 'til late at night. I didn't have a problem with any of that. Every time he invited me to some place I went. After 6 months, our relationship changed. He didn't call me as often, but he still took me out and it appeared he still loved me.

One day, he said he needed time because he was confused, and he didn't know if he loved me as a friend or a girlfriend. We were both crying. With great pain, I gave him time to decide what he wanted and he said he would call me.

Two months passed, and I didn't see or hear from him. I was worried because I hoped we would be together again. Then my best friend ran into him. She asked him why he hadn't called me. He told her he was embarrassed to tell me his mother threw him out of his house because he made his ex-girlfriend pregnant, and now he has to get married. I couldn't imagine he would do that to me.

He finally came to my house and we talked. He told me he loved this other girl. I didn't understand because I thought he loved me. We are supposed to be friends now, but he told me he couldn't call or visit me because he was married.

I am writing to you because I think all this is my fault because I didn't go to bed with him. That's why he made that other girl pregnant. I don't know what to do without him. I loved him, and I still do.

Please help me. Please give me advice about how I can go on with my life, knowing I will never have him again. I don't want to become sick because of this problem. I can't go on with my life. I want to be happy again, but knowing he's with another woman tears my heart out.

Elisa

Dear Elisa,

This guy chose to sleep with someone else, even after he made those empty promises to you. When a guy loves a girl, he respects her and supports her wishes. He doesn't run out and make another girl pregnant. And if he really loved this other girl, he would have been man enough to be responsible and use protection.

It's a good thing you did not choose to have sex with him! If he had been sleeping with other girls and you, too, all without protection, who knows what kind of diseases he could have given you. And of course, he could have made you pregnant, also. Nice guy he is!!

The universe protected you by giving this dude to someone else. Of course, you are hurt because you wonder how you could have been such a fool to fall for his lies. Women much older than you contact me after being left with a lifetime disease *and* a baby!

Women blame themselves because they think it's their job to make their relationships work. That's not true. This guy cheated on you and encouraged you to care for him, without being honest. There's no excuse for that.

Be without any guy for a while to get yourself together. You will recover from this and be so thankful. Please let me know how you're doing.
Dr. Gilda

Dear Dr. Gilda,

I am writing to thank you very much. I really needed to hear your words. I will try to go on, and you bet I am not going to be with another guy for a while. I realize I need time for me. If it's okay with you, I will keep letting you know how I'm doing.

Again, thank you. I didn't know there would be someone like you, so interested in helping young women the way you have helped me.
Elisa

Always say "no" with grace to things you don't want. Love begins with a girl's respect for herself.

The Respect Connect

Just as girls should command respect from guys, they must first respect themselves. Like the differences in our hormones, brains, and bodies, the two genders want respect in different ways. Girls want to be cherished and appreciated for kind, caring, and attractive. Guys want respect from girls for excelling at an activity they perform.

Guys enjoy having their girlfriends watch them win a basketball game. They crave their girlfriends' praise for having negotiated a great raise at work. They love it when their girlfriend makes it a big deal when they ace a tough test. Guys want to feel like heroes in the eyes of their ladies.

DON'T LIE ON YOUR BACK . . .

<u>How Do I Communicate with My Guy?</u>

Being a hero in his lady's eyes is one thing, but the stuff that makes a relationship work involves honest and truthful communication. As with respect, honesty has to work both ways. Girls who want a cool guy, yet lie to the one they've got eventually get what they deserve.

Dear Dr. Gilda,

My new boyfriend thinks I'm older than I am. I don't know how to tell him the truth. I'm 16, and he's 5 years older than I am. I'm afraid if he finds out he'll get really mad. We haven't been going out long, but I need some advice to tell him the truth, without having him hate me. What should I do?
Sharon

Dear Sharon,

Open your mouth, look your guy in the eyes, and say these words, "I'm sorry, but I'm younger than you think I am. I'm 16, not 19." If your boyfriend is angry you lied to him, it would not be surprising. No relationship built on lies can last. Besides, at 16, if he had sex with you, he could be incarcerated.

The quicker you level with him, the better. And it's best that you do it yourself, before he hears the truth from a third party. Every action has a consequence, and it's time you faced up to yours.
Dr. Gilda

Girls must be honest with their guys, so when it's their turn to receive, they'll get honesty back.

Gilda-Gram®
What we give out,
we get back.

Usually, guys are not apt to spill their guts or display their weak spots. Neither will they talk for hours on the phone, as girls do. So don't think you will replace your girlfriends for a boyfriend.

Even if your relationship starts out romantic, most guys prefer to join sporting events or hang with their friends, not talk to you about sensitive topics. Cavemen didn't return to the cave to woo and coo their women. It Girls don't take these behaviors personally; they accept them.

If your guy is suddenly acting distant with you, before you accuse him of cheating make him feel safe to open up about what's bugging him. Understand this is difficult for him because he never wants to appear "less than a man" in your eyes. He won't be open with you, unless he's certain you won't tease him about his sensitivity, and that you won't gossip about his personal problems to your friends. Trust takes time, and he'll need to be certain he can trust you with his special feelings.

Maggie saw that Barry was beginning to withdraw from their relationship. She was certain there was no one else he was interested in. But she couldn't get him to tell her what was on his mind.

Finally, she blurted out that she was having a family problem she had been keeping private. Her father was an alcoholic and after some tumultuous fights with her mom, her parents were divorcing. This was ripping Maggie apart. She felt so close to Barry she confided this to him. Suddenly, he felt more bonded to her.

Crises can either bring a couple closer or rip them apart. Once Maggie confided in him, Barry revealed his mom and dad were also getting divorced. He was glad he had someone to share his grief with!

Gilda-Gram®
Trust is based on openness.

What's the best way to have good communication? Declare your expectations in one clear statement. Don't criticize him for not calling after he promised he would. Guys are very sensitive to a woman's judgments, and you don't want your crush to wonder whether he's speaking to his critical mom.

Dear Dr. Gilda,
I am 23, and have had my boyfriend for 4 months. Things were absolutely great in the beginning. But now each time we text, we have trouble saying things to each other. Hanging out with him and seeing him at school is amazing.

I don't know how to "rekindle" what we had. I have to do it soon, before I lose him. He decided to work at the same camp as me during the summer. That's not making me happy.
Lindsay

Dear Lindsay,

It is possible you're very attracted to each other, so when you are face-to-face firecrackers blast. But when you are texting, you may be discovering you don't share a lot of common interests.

Maybe you're becoming bored with each other, since you said you're not thrilled he'll be working with you during the summer. Or maybe he's ready to move back to spending more time with the guys.

Even though you're not excited he'll be at your summer camp, you say you don't want to lose him. Girl, what exactly do you want?

Gilda-Gram®
**The fear of losing a guy
should never be the reason to stay with him.**

At first, all relationships begin as hot romances. But what sustains a good relationship over time is deep communicate. The communication problem you're having after this short time is telling you something about your future. Open your eyes to the truth.
Dr. Gilda

Since girls are usually better communicators than guys, study these 8 Tips to get your guy to open his sensitive side.

8 Tips To Pry the Often-Shy

1. Since guys generally don't feel comfortable sharing their feelings, especially at the beginning of a

relationship, ask your guy what he *thinks* about something, not what he *feels* about it.

2. Since guys are goal-driven, encourage your guy to describe what he *did*, not how he *felt*. Get him to *describe* it and *listen enthusiastically* so he'll realize you care.

3. If you want to find out his views on love, discuss the breakup of mutual friends. Solicit his thoughts about the situation, which will imply his feelings.

4. Since guys are not as talkative as you and your friends, ask open-ended questions that begin with "How?" and "Why?" Avoid questions that require just a one-word response.

5. Since guys have the rep for being such poor listeners, invite his opinions as you share something with him.

6. Don't ever think your guy will give you detailed information like your girlfriends. Girls blab with intricate information far more than boys.

7. Decode what he really means. It's tough for a guy to tell you he loves you. Instead, he may criticize the dorky guy who hangs out with you. Or he may tell you the gorgeous hunk you laugh with is not so cute. Although he's not saying much, he's implying plenty.

8. Prove to your guy you will keep his mushy words just between the two of you. If you blow his cover, he'll never trust you again.

Since we spend a lot of time talking, we all think

we know how to communicate. When you follow these 8 Tips, you're on your way to getting your guy to begin communicating more.

Being a good communicator takes practice, as you'll see with the "Comfortable Communication Quiz."

Comfortable Communication Quiz

Beside each question, write Yes or No.

____ 1. Do I communicate easily with my guy?

____ 2. Do I know about his family?

____ 3. Do I worry about feeling stupid when I'm with him?

____ 4. Do I know what he's interested in?

____ 5. Do I know how to make him laugh?

____ 6. Do I know what makes him sad?

____ 7. Do I freely share my feelings with him?

____ 8. Do I feel "safe" communicating with him, knowing he won't tease or embarrass me?

ScoreCard

<u>1 - 3 Yeses:</u> You're like strangers now, and you need to get to know each other better before you believe you're an item.

<u>4 - 5 Yeses:</u> As well as you think you know each other, you still need to become more comfortable and open.

<u>6 - 8 Yeses:</u> You've got the makings of a rosy future. Whatever you're doing, keep it up.

Karlie took the "Comfortable Communication Quiz," and found she scored 4 Yeses. When we started to talk about her score, she admitted she still needed to feel "safe" around her boyfriend of three months. He continued to embarrass her with her friends, which made her uncomfortable. When asked to describe an embarrassing event, she said:

"Brad is super great to me and sweet and everything. I truly love him with all my heart, and he knows it. But he's been frustrating me lately because he always asks for my friends' screen names. When I give them to him, he goes straight to his email and curses them out. He knows I wouldn't leave him, so he doesn't care what he does.

I told him to stop doing that to people. He's not a bad guy, but he won't leave my friends alone. Now, most of my friends hate him! I don't want to leave him, but I'm wondering if backing off for a while might help him realize I'm REALLY sick of it."

I explained to Karlie that respect for her wishes is a very important trait of a cool boyfriend. Although she thinks Brad is "super great" to her, he has dissed her wishes—and that's disrespectful!!

I also told her I was concerned she couldn't say

"no" to him when he asked for the screen names of her friends. I said, "If you can't say 'no' to Brad for a small request like this, what will happen when he asks you to do something you find really nasty?"

I said this example shows how she must know what she wants, be willing to speak her mind, and decide what she's prepared to do if Brad trashes her wishes. As long as she's not honest with him about her feelings, she'll be agreeing to things that are not coming from her heart. And she'll never feel safe communicating with this dude.

Taking this "Comfortable Communication Quiz" was Karlie's wake-up call that if Brad was not respecting her wishes, she'd have to abandon her vow never to leave him. Finally, she knew she had to begin by learning to say "no."

Saying "No" Makes You Feel Good

Saying "no" is a difficult chore for most females, young and old. Being the nurturers we are, we don't want our friends to feel bad, we don't want to gain enemies, we want to be liked, and we don't want to ruin the relationships that mean so much to us. Somehow, we mistakenly think it's our female obligation to keep peace.

This makes us people pleasers, not just with guys, but with everyone we meet. By not being totally frank, we give away a part of ourselves. Then we naturally become angry, upset, and stressed about being pushed to the limit.

However, instead of being angry with ourselves for allowing this, we become angry with our parents, our friends, or our boyfriends.

Gilda-Gram®
We are responsible for our own actions.

Every action we take has a consequence of some kind. So the first promise a young woman must make is with herself.

Gilda-Gram®
Agree not to go along to get along.

If you lie to yourself or accept shabby treatment just to be accepted into the "in" crowd, your self-esteem will plummet. Visualize standing on your own in an open field. Breathe in the free air, and realize how terrific it is not to have to answer to people whose values you don't share.

Gilda-Gram®
**If a guy doesn't respect your wishes,
he doesn't respect you.**

It may be tough to accept you have to dump a guy because he doesn't have your back. But it's better you find out sooner, not later. Once you discover he's gotta go, be grateful you came to your senses as soon as you did. Then make plans to move on.

Life has a funny way of rewarding us for making

the right decision. After you've dumped the guy who's been giving you so much grief, watch who comes strolling your way. It's some *new* dude who's cooler than cool. As soon as you meet him, you'll wonder what you ever saw in your old crush.

How would you respond to this scenario? Steve's parents are going to be away for the weekend, and Steve has planned a big bash at his house. You know Steve's friends are part of the fast crowd at school, and you also know your parents would kill you if they found out you were partying where there are drugs, sex, and alcohol. They've grounded you in the past for less, and you're sure you would not be allowed out forever if you got caught.

You're crazy about Steve and you are so glad he finally asked you out. He's begging you to come. What do you do?

We've all wanted to be somewhere we couldn't be. It makes us feel bad we're missing all the fun. Of course, you're bummed because you know you'll have to decline Steve's invitation. But how do you do it in a way that will communicate you're still interested in him?

5 Strategies to Turn Him Down without Turning Him Off

1. Remind yourself you have the right to say "no," and the obligation to be true to yourself and your values. Sure, your values may be those forced on you by

your parents, but you're the one who will suffer the consequences if your folks find out you lied.

2. Suggest an alternate plan to get together. For example, say, "Steve, I'd love to go to your party, but my folks will ground me for life if they find out your parents won't be home. Instead, can we get together after school next week?" So you turn him down, without *letting* him down.

3. Don't be drawn into your crush's pleading. A guy who pressures you to change your mind with, "Your parents will never find out" or "If you don't come to the party, I'll have to ask another girl" does not have your back. All he's saying is that he cares solely about his desires, and he demands you do whatever it takes to satisfy them. This kind of guy doesn't want a girlfriend; he wants a puppet!

Dear Dr. Gilda,
        Why are men such babies?
Elizabeth

Dear Elizabeth,
        Men are such babies because we women baby them!
Dr. Gilda

<u>**Gilda-Gram®**</u>
**If a guy you turn down
threatens to find someone else,
tell him to go ahead!**

4. Use the 3 Be's: *Be* brief. *Be* friendly. *Be*

firm. If you even hint you might change your mind, your guy will try to change it for you. Follow the 3 Be's, then disengage your eye contact, turn your body away, or change the subject. He'll know the case is closed.

5. If it's still tough for you to say "no" to a guy you're crushing on, buy time. Time buying is easy, if you use one of these statements:

- "I don't think my folks will let me, but I'll ask them anyway.

- "I have to study now. Let's discuss this later."

- "The party's not until next Friday. I have a week to work on my parents. I'll let you know."

Gilda-Gram®
**Time-buying techniques de-stress you,
while you decide how to proceed.**

At first, if you're not used to it, saying "no" to people you'd rather say "yes" to could be a challenge. Some people won't want to accept your "no." Others may take your rejection personally and call you names. Remember your strong inner self. Make your decision and stick to your guns!

After you've mastered these principles, you'll begin to feel better about yourself and your ability to communicate your boundaries. Communicating your boundaries shows others how you respect yourself and teaches them to respect you, too.

Dear Dr. Gilda,

I just broke up with my boyfriend because he often calls me a slut. I'm fed up with it. He's not taking the breakup well. How can I tell him I'm sick of his behavior?

I don't want to be mean or nasty the way he is. I just want to be straightforward about how I feel.
Jill

Dear Jill,

It's wonderful to hear from such a mature young woman. It's good you don't want to roll in the mud with your former guy.

Apparently, he believed you would accept his poor treatment indefinitely. That's why he can't believe you dumped him now. Tough!

Make your comments short and sweet. Deliver your message, change the subject, or walk away. He'll understand his begging and pleading will do him no good.

<u>Gilda-Gram®</u>
**There's a lot of love
in saying "no."**

The love in the word "no" is the respect you have for YOU. Go for it, girl. Goal for it, It Girl. I applaud you!
Dr. Gilda

People who demonstrate they care about themselves send the message they can care about others.

<u>Gilda-Gram®</u>
**When you say--and mean—"I love *me*,"
you are able to say--and mean—"I love *you*."**

All people go through ups and downs. Teens have drastic highs and lows because their hormones take a continuous roller-coaster ride. Understanding these hormonal spurts makes it easier to forgive bizarre behavior. But there is never an excuse for putting up with disrespect. To attract only the best treatment:

1. Know what you want.

2. Establish your boundaries.

3. Communicate your boundaries.

4. Accept *only* the best treatment.

5. Be prepared to walk away if you don't get what you want.

A worthy guy shows he's terrific because he demonstrates 3 C's:

1) Character

2) Compassion

3) Commitment.

Character gives him backbone to stand up to his goofy friends when they tell him he's acting too mushy with you. Compassion gives him the capacity to be happy when showing he cares. Commitment shows you can depend on him, and trust him to be honest and watch your back.

<u>Gilda-Gram®</u>
You deserve
to be honored and adored.

NEED #3

Pursue Your Happy Places

Someone once told us that when it comes to love, two halves make a whole. So we've mistakenly believed each of us has a "missing piece" and someone else will provide the stuff we lack. It's a continuation of the fairy tales that taught young women that "someday my prince will come" and *he'll* make us better than we actually are.

Many girls think they are not capable, rich, funny, beautiful, thin, or intelligent enough on their own. They imagine an all-powerful guy will get them to transform from yucky duckling into graceful swan. They especially believe he'll remove their feelings of emptiness and low self-esteem.

In the movie, Jerry McGuire, Jerry told his girlfriend, "You complete me." I hear many girls confess they're scared to be alone, and they *need*--mind you, *need*--a boyfriend to fill their loneliness, and make them feel pretty. Newsflash: No one can "complete" someone else.

That is not to say that people don't

unconsciously look for mates with opposite traits. Opposites do attract. But if they're not the right *kind* of opposites, over time they repel. For example, a person with a lively personality will attract a quieter mate. That's a good thing because it would be impossible for two big mouths to compete for airtime!

In contrast to the more obvious personality traits, character traits lie beneath the surface. What are your likes? What makes you joyful? What are your goals? These have nothing to do with your cute crush donning the coolest clothes or having the whitest smile. Those surface traits wear thin quickly. But values and beliefs go much deeper. Because they're so deep, when they're well matched they form a bond that lasts.

For example, if your crush values smoking weed and you don't, he may pressure you to conform to his values, believing you're too square the way you are. Meanwhile, you may begin pressuring him to stop smoking weed. Pressures that each person puts on the other can derail a relationship.

Dear Dr. Gilda,
I have been with my boyfriend for 5 months. He's real good-looking, and he's got a great body. But now I'm fed up with his sloppy eating habits.

Whenever we go to a restaurant, food drips down his face and onto his clothes. It's embarrassing! I really thought I loved him, but now I'm not so sure. What should I do?
Alicia

Dear Alicia,

Girls must get to know a guy well before committing to loving him. Although you're a neater eater than your guy, this superficial difference is starting to gnaw at you. And it's only been five months into the relationship!

It's a good thing you are getting to know him in a lot of different situations. Remember the "Make-a-Choice Quiz"? Return to it and see if you really want to keep this guy around.

What bugs you about his behavior may be all right for another girl. But your feelings are *your* feelings and you're entitled to them. Finding out about different people's traits is why it's important to date a variety of guys before you commit to one.

Gilda-Gram®
**Dating is just practice
for lasting love.**

Your heart will tell you whether to accept your guy as is or dump him and his sloppy food intake.
Dr. Gilda

The Benefit of Becoming Whole

At any time, your alleged Prince Charming can get sloppy, get sick, or leave. Where would that leave you? Clearly, every young woman must start out by being her *own* rescuer!

In love, two halves do NOT make a whole. Vow to become a complete person, enjoying all your activities to their fullest, before you seek a mate. If you're dependent on a guy to complete you, remember that he's got his own problems and he doesn't need or even want yours.

Gilda-Gram®
A boyfriend doesn't make you complete.
YOU make you complete.

Of course, if you already have a boyfriend, it's never too late to start taking care of yourself. If you're with a guy who's too demanding, controlling, or restricting and you've changed yourself to please him, wise up.

What do *you* want to do? If you don't do what you want, you're being dishonest. If you're being dishonest, you're attracting someone who's settling for less of a girl. That's *not* a cool guy. The more honest you are, the more easily you'll attract the *right* guy.

Gilda-Gram®
Being whole
attracts the coolest guys.

Because we attract who we are, when we invest in ourselves we attract mates who are invested in themselves, too. Your new guy might even be that once unobtainable dude! Together you can form a *partnership*. Partnership beats *hero worship,* with you crushing on him but not getting your feelings returned.

When two *partners* join forces, each has the other's back, and love is natural and flowing.

The Need to Chill Solo

No matter how busy you are and how committed you want to be to your friends, school, job, family, or guy, it's vital you schedule time for YOU in your happiest places. That may mean just texting your friends. Or making time to do absolutely nothing. Solo time is when no one interferes in your space to dictate rules that aren't yours.

There are plenty of benefits of chilling solo. Even in small doses, goofing off lets you freely dream your dreams. If you want to believe you'll be the next class president, here is where you'll entertain that vision. If you want to fantasize becoming a famous recording artist, this is the magical place.

Sit in your room, go to the beach, grab a glimpse of sunset, or envision walking on a cloud and feeling the marshmallowy pillows beneath your toes. Sing, dance, moan, or groan. Take a nap. Chill time is yours to do what you want.

While you're chilling solo, do the "Best Bud Tune-Up." Earlier, we discussed the traits of good friends. When you're growing, your friendships change and you need to continue to reassess them.

Best Bud Tune-Up

Answer Yes to either 1) or 2) below:

___1. Do my best friends defend me and bend for me?

OR

___2. Do my best friends drain me and pain me?

ScoreCard

If you answered Yes to Question 1, you've got good friends. If you answered Yes to Question 2, you need to edit your friendship list. Replace draining friends with more caring ones.

Another chill-out solo activity is to assess the studly guy you're gushing over. Is your cutie crushing back? If some mean friends badmouth you, would he have your back and defend you?

Having a boyfriend requires that you let him know the real you. It's important you both honestly open up.

Crush-on-You Quiz

Answer Yes or No to each of the following:

___1. Does he remember your birthday and other important occasions?

___2. Does he accompany you to dull family outings?

169

___3. Does he call to say he misses you?

___4. Does he stick to plans you've made?

___5. Does he show obvious signs he's over his ex?

___6. Does he say nice things about you when you're not around?

___7. Does he go out of his way to see you?

ScoreCard

<u>5 - 7 Yeses:</u> This cutie's crushing back big time!

<u>3 - 4 Yeses:</u> Maybe he's missed your signs and needs more encouragement. There is interest, but you'll have to do more fishing before reeling this trout in.

<u>1 - 2 Yeses:</u> You're experiencing hero worship. If your crush doesn't return your feelings, it's time to find a cuter cutie that will.

You learn things about yourself and your relationships when you are solo. Enjoy every moment!

Take A Breather
After a Breakup

Ginny was devastated. She had just been dumped by Charlie whom she had been seeing for two years. The breakup came as a big shock to her because she thought things were fine between them.

About a year earlier, he had bought her a cell phone. She obeyed his request to call him every hour.

She also gave into sex whenever he wanted it. When he told her she couldn't hang out with her girlfriend Joan, she obeyed that, too. When he told her to wear less makeup, she agreed. When he screamed at her for wearing a skirt he said was too short, she peeled it off. She thought she was the ideal girlfriend and that he'd never leave.

At first, guys who control girls enjoy the power. But after a girl becomes her guy's trained seal, he tends to get bored.

Suddenly, without warning, Charlie told the 19-year-old he didn't want to have a steady girlfriend any more. He said he felt tied down. That was on a Friday. On Saturday, he was spotted escorting a popular girl to the movies. Ginny cried for days.

A breakup can be torture for some people. But scientists find that most people deal with breakups pretty well, and even actually thrive in personal growth as a result of the split. But they must mourn the loss, and assess what really happened and what their role in the breakup was. If they do this constructively, they will conclude their ex is not the only person they will love, and that they can look forward to falling in love again.

Mourning is mandatory after you lose someone. Some girls run from one romance to another, without understanding what went wrong. That's not a good idea because every situation teaches a lesson.

Gilda-Gram®
**After every high and every low,
ask yourself, "What did I learn?"**

Unless we assess the mistakes we made,
including why we fell for a guy who was disrespectful,
we're likely to repeat the same errors with a new guy.
Sure, a new guy might look different, sound different,
and be different from the guy we left behind, but he'll
have the same difficult qualities we never learned to deal
with in our past. Every lost love teaches great lessons!

Gilda-Gram®
**Relationships are less about finding love,
and more about finding YOU.**

Learning about yourself includes making
mistakes, falling apart, learning your lessons, getting
stronger, getting smarter, and moving on. This is
growth. Being joyful is part of growth, but so is having
heartache.

As much as I'd love to tell you otherwise, we
learn more about ourselves from our lows than we do
from our highs. And unfortunately, when it comes to
being sad, there are no shortcuts. We must all do the
necessary self-growth work, like taking the quizzes in
this book and analyzing their results.

Gilda-Gram®
**The only way *out* of pain is *through* pain.
Feel each feeling deeply so you can let it go.**

To be able to let your feelings go, follow the "3-Step Take Care Plan."

3-Step Take Care Plan

1. <u>Get Busy</u>. Join your school paper, register for tennis lessons, or volunteer at the local hospital. Do anything to take your mind off your breakup.

2. <u>Get Solo</u>. *Some* amount of feeling sorry for yourself is all right. But put a cap on how long you'll permit yourself to drown in your tears. Say, "I'm giving myself one hour to cry. After that, I'm going to study for tomorrow's math test." Then chant this

Gilda-Gram®
For **a while, I'll mope.**
After **a while, I'll cope.**

3. <u>Get Friendly</u>. Good friends that passed the "Best Bud Tune-Up" will listen to you go on about the crush that crashed. Haven't you done the same for them when they were suffering? Review the part you played in the breakup, and vow that the next mistakes you make will not be repeats of this one.

Gilda-Gram®
Let your *next* mistakes
be *new* mistakes.

After a breakup, many girls would rather be surrounded by people, instead of being alone. But crowds won't dull your pain. You must always return to your solo place and process what happened so it will not happen again.

If you schedule time in advance and follow the "moping-then-coping" Gilda-Gram® for feeling better, you can map out the way you'll spend your next few weeks.

You may hate your guy because of the way he treated you. But if you're hating, you're still feeling.

Gilda-Gram®
Hate is not the opposite of love.
Indifference is.

Until you are totally *indifferent* to what your ex did, what he's doing now, and even who he's dating, you're not over him, and you need more time to mend.

Everyone needs a different amount of time to heal. Sally Ann spent six months mourning the end of a one-year relationship, but Nettie needed only three weeks. To get totally over him and to accelerate your healing process, uplift *YOU*. Make your happy places your new romantic interests.

Warning! It's human nature to feel that since you can't *have* him back, you want to *get* him back—by making him jealous, stalking him, or worse. Forget it! Perish your evil thoughts because you'll only make a fool of yourself when you find he doesn't care.

Gilda-Gram®
The best revenge is doing well.

174

Doing well involves getting into your own life and excelling at the things you love. Most It Girls have graduated from the Been-There-Done-That School of Grief before they realized it was time to take charge.

Pump Up Your Passions

Interest*ing* chicas are interest*ed* chicas. While some girls chase guys, It Girls chase their dreams. This makes it challenging for the guys interested in them to get their attention.

The things people work hard for are valued more. If It Girls are pursuing their passions rather than pursuing the guys other girls want, whom do you think the guys are interested in? Not the easy ones!

Passion is contagious. When you're passionate about something you love to do, a guy will become passionate about you. Attraction is that simple!

Passion Assessment

What do you love doing that's very special to you?

_____

To succeed at your passions, squash your fears about what others think. Stand tall, raise your chin, uncross your arms, smile, and act approachable. Get a new hairstyle, a new outfit, or different makeup. But be careful your motive for your new-and-improved self is *only to make yourself fresher and better than you've ever been.* It's not to re-snag your ex.

You are the only one who counts now. If your ex cared about you, he wouldn't be your ex.

Gilda-Gram®
Getting him back
will not move you forward.

Once you're on the right path, you'll feel it. Then one day out of the blue, a friend will mention X's name. Without hesitation you'll reply, "X who?" Your response might surprise you, but you'll know this dude is history.

Finding Guys Online

Getting to know someone well before you meet face-to-face is one way to prevent physical *dis*traction. Online encounters could be a good method for meeting guys if you're shy. But many girls foolishly feel safe about sharing personal information with an online stranger, thinking he could never jump through the computer screen and harm them.

But a girl can't know whether the person on the other side of the screen is the one he claims to be. He says he's a 19-year-old guy, but he could be an older man or woman. He claims to be in college, but he could be a criminal in another country.

Dear Dr. Gilda,
I am 14 and in love with someone I met online. I will be able to meet him this summer, and he wants to have sex. What should I do?

Willie

Dear Willie,

You must be kidding! I receive a lot of emails from unsuspecting girls like you who think some character online is okay. Despite the tender words he writes, don't fall for it! Behind the computer screen, a guy could tell you anything. Most people pump up their social media resumes to appear better than they really are. I hear horror stories from females of all ages who were hurt badly by a guy they met online.

Maybe the guy you've met is okay, although I doubt it since he already told you he wants to have sex on your first meeting. If you tell him you're *not* interested in sex, would he be just as anxious to meet?

You mention your age, but you don't know his. There have been murders from online meetings. Get some guidance from an adult you trust.
Dr. Gilda

Questions like Willie's upset me. She is young and trusting. I want to run workshops in It Girl Training. It Girls know their value and they won't put up with nonsense!

Dear Dr. Gilda,

I met this guy online two months ago. The relationship went fast. He asked me to marry him and I said "yes." We will meet in June. But now he is not so attentive and not as charming as he used to be. Perhaps he is too sure of me. I also think he is not being honest about how he spends his time.

I am confused and I can't talk to him about this. What am I to do?
Online Girl

Dear Online,
How lucky you didn't meet this dude yet! You rushed things so fast, in two months you were ready to walk down the aisle for the rest of your life!!

This character is beginning to show his true colors. You want to ask him questions, but you "can't talk to him" about them. Yet you'd marry him???

You already suspect he's not being honest. You can't marry someone you don't trust. Run fast!! Hopefully, you have seen the light!
Dr. Gilda

Flush Away the Bad Boy

I receive tons of email from girls who are wild about "bad boys." They're the guys who steal your heart, can't be trusted, lie, cheat, and diss you every chance they get. They're no Prince Charmings! Although these baddies are enticing, few are nice.

Dear Dr. Gilda,
Earlier I wrote to you about being desperate for one of two different guys. Well, the one who's free still ignores me, but today for some reason, the one who's taken was a total flirt! There is a dance coming up at school and he said he would dance with me and my two other buddies. I felt great--until I found out he might dump his girl for my friend. I am so jealous.

How can I show him a good time at the dance and win him away without her knowing? Of course, if she went out with him, she would still be a good friend. She doesn't know he likes her yet and I don't want her to know. I have a week until this dance. Is there something I can do at school? Help me!
Lost With Love

Dear Lost With Love,
I don't like that you're feeling "desperate" for love. But why would you want either of these two turkeys? One doesn't know you're breathing, and the other flirts with everyone in skirts.

When you pursue unavailable dudes, you're saying you're willing to take *anyone*. Really?

Gilda-Gram®
If love's a game,
you don't need it.

Love is beautiful, but you'll never know if you continue to set yourself up for heartache with the wrong guys.
Dr. Gilda

Gilda-Gram®
Don't long to be part of *a* couple.
Long to be part of *the right* couple.

Experts say it takes 21 days to kill a habit. Affairs of the heart may take longer. But like giving up smoking, it's worth the hassle.

179

When you're ready to say goodbye to someone not treating you right, say, "Self, no matter how he begs or what he says, this relationship is o-v-e-r."

To be sure you're not tempted, screen your calls, take alternate routes to school and work so you won't run into him, and follow the 3-Step Take Care Plan: Get Busy, Get Solo, Get Friendly.

As you begin to move on without him, of course you'll feel the emptiness. You weren't crazy. There were some good reasons you liked him. But,

Gilda-Gram®
Feeling the blues, like feeling hungry, is only a temporary condition.

Bad boys aren't interested in watching anyone's back but their own. They make girls feel horrible. They do things that are unacceptable, illegal, and immoral.

You can tell from what bad boys say, how they look, and what they wear that you should keep your distance. Sometimes they will be withdrawn and moody. Other times, they will be hostile and angry.

These are obvious personality types and looks to avoid. But these can be deceiving. A guy at my gym has giant biceps, is obviously taking steroids, and his body is painted with colorful tattoos. He looks like a real bad boy. BUT, he told me he teaches yoga, and his plain-looking wife comes to the gym, too, and they often discuss their baby!

Other bad boys look like the boy next door, yet

deliver sweet lines that would make any girl swoon. These Romeos have their badness down to a science, and naive girls flip for them. Don't let that happen to you.

Dear Dr. Gilda,

I recently made out with my friend's 20-year-old brother. Could he have feelings for me, even though he's 7 years older than I am? Or is he just using me? Help!!
Jaime

Dear Jaime,

There are laws that make it illegal for this guy to be hooking up with a minor. He could be arrested.

He's much too old for you, and of course he's taking advantage of your innocence, which you already know or you wouldn't be asking this question. What could a 13-year-old talk about with a *man* of 20? But now that I've used the word "man," I must reconsider. Is he immature, immoral, or just plain stupid?

I know it feels great to attract an older guy. But there's something wrong with him if he thinks he can have a relationship with someone your age. In a few years, the difference in your ages won't matter. But for now the law protects you against your own immaturity. Please, please find a guy more appropriate so you won't get used or hurt.
Dr. Gilda

This guy is the brother of someone Jaime calls a "friend." Presumably, her friend knows Jaime and her brother connected. Jaime should be very cautious because surely her friend doesn't have her back.

From this example, we learn that no matter how terrific your friends may seem or how sweet and appropriate a guy may appear,

Gilda-Gram®
You must watch your *own* back!

Of course you want a guy to help protect your back. But no one will look out for you the way you look out for yourself. And a guy won't even know how to look out for you—unless you show him!

Become your own caretaker, your own protector. This is what It Girls do. By sharpening your awareness, you will be able to identify the characteristics of a bad boy.

Everybody makes mistakes. Even It Girls sometimes miss the signs. But guys who have no regard for their steady girlfriends or the children they father are dangerous. Keeping these guys around is NOT the way to create excitement in your life.

Dear Dr. Gilda,
I really hope you can help me give a friend a wake-up call. Carole is 19 and dating this guy who has a live-in girlfriend with a child. Carole has been seeing him for two years and he has been telling her how bad things are with his girlfriend. He started seeing my friend before he moved in with the other one.

At the beginning, they went everywhere together

and he was very loving. Recently, he started neglecting Carole. To compete with the other girl, Carole got her own apartment in hopes he would start spending more time with her. Well, it didn't work.

Now she wants to have his baby, although she insists it's not to compete with the other girl. She says she wants a baby, even if he doesn't, as long as he will spend time with his child as it grows. When I told her to look for someone who cares for her, she responded that things were good enough for her as they were.

Dr. Gilda, I have tried to give my advice. But it's not what she wants to hear and she has completely shut me out. This is not her first bad boy relationship. She had spent 5 years with a married man.

She mopes around, hoping this guy will show up. Please help. I don't want to see her get hurt.
Gisele

Dear Gisele,
Carole is a mess, and the best thing she's got is YOU. As much as you try to reason with her, it does no good. I can understand how frustrated you feel. If she thinks a baby will keep this guy around, she's setting herself up for a bigger letdown.

Girls who continually seek bad boys don't believe they are good enough to attract a cool guy who can love them. This is Carole's pattern and nothing you do will change her.

You can't help someone who doesn't want to be helped. You're not your friend's teacher or preacher.

Get on with your life and let Carole learn on her own that friends like you are golden, and bad boys don't change.
Dr. Gilda

I get thousands of emails from girls who *refuse* to heed the bad boy warnings and insist they *still love him!! Duhhhhhh!!*

Dear Dr. Gilda,
My boyfriend broke up with me a week ago. We had been going out for 6 months. He says I didn't treat him special enough. But really he's the one with the problem. I did more for him than he ever did for me. Then he mentally abused me. But I still love him and want him back. What should I do?
Jane

Dear Jane,
This guy mentally abused you, gave you little compassion, and complained you didn't do enough for him? Sorry, but he doesn't need a girlfriend; he needs a nipple. Nobody will ever be able to make him happy.

Many girls get into your situation, misbelieving that if only they could make their miserable boyfriend happy, they'd be happy, too. The more they try to change themselves, the less they respect themselves . . . and, the less their guy respects them.

Gilda-Gram®
People who love you
don't hurt you.

How can you love a guy who mentally abuses you, gives you little to go on, and then complains you're not giving enough? As much as you claim the problem lies with him, you get the prize for stupidity for wanting him back ANYWAY! Get a life, girl!!
Dr. Gilda

Dear Dr. Gilda,
I have known and liked this guy for 7 months. He wanted to keep it friends because he's a bad boy and he thought I was too "good." Well, we have this thing going where we have "fun" in private, but we don't tell anyone because he doesn't want to be tied down right now.

I know I am not the only girl he's seeing, but I am the one who he knows the best. I really like him and I can't get him off my mind. I know he likes me as a friend and maybe more. What should I do to make a move he can't refuse? I can be exactly what he wants.
Stephanie

Dear Stephanie,
Exactly what kind of move "he can't refuse" did you have in mind? Let's say you make that "move." Sorry, girl, but that still won't keep him!

What scares me is your statement that you're willing to become "exactly what he wants." Are you a blob of clay?

Right now, this guy likes you, but is using you for secret sex while also getting it elsewhere. You need a guy willing to invite you into his life—and be proud to

let the world know. With the right guy you don't have to redecorate yourself.
Dr. Gilda

Dear Dr. Gilda,
        I really like this guy I work with, but he is always mean to me. Usually, he doesn't talk to me at all. Help me, please.
Rosemary

Dear Rosemary,
        Please fill me in with exactly what you like about someone mean to you who also ignores you.
How can you say you even *know* him or even *like* him? Would you befriend a girlfriend that treated you this way? Get real!
Dr. Gilda

        These girls want unavailable guys because they are not secure in believing they deserve more. They put up with horrendous treatment or they attempt to make themselves irreplaceable by becoming the guy's nurse. They think if they "save" him from himself, he'll be forever grateful and stay. *He won't!*

Dear Dr. Gilda,
        I see you on TV all the time, and you are great. I am dating this guy I like very much. He is 19 and I'm 18. He's sweet and treats me with respect. The only thing is that he doesn't go to school and he smokes weed. I think by being around him I can change him because when he's with me he doesn't do it.

        My boyfriend says he wants to do something

with his life. But when is he going to start? He's
already 19 and doesn't have a high school diploma. I'm
trying to talk him into getting his GED. How can I get it
through his head that he needs an education? I don't
know why I fall for these guys!
Ginger

Dear Ginger,
        The only question you should be asking is the
last: Why do I fall for these guys? Trying to be a savior
to your boyfriend is taking focus away from what you
must do with your life. You are right; when is this guy
going to grow up?

        The answer to your question is that you feel best
when your guy needs you. Give that up! You already
wasted too much time on this loser.
Dr. Gilda

        What do these girls like--or love--about these
guys? Although Stephanie was interested in making "a
move he can't refuse," she's already putting her body on
the line for a guy who's not interested. This never
works.

        What else would Stephanie like to do to prove
she cares? Steal? Rob? Murder?? These guys escort
these girls into relationship hell. *But it's the girls who
agree to stay there.*

Gilda-Gram®
**The question is not what's wrong
with your bad boy.
It's *what's wrong with you
for staying with him???***

It's always easy to point the finger of blame at the boys for being bad. But,

<u>Gilda-Gram®</u>
Bad boys don't *take* from girls.
They are *given*.

A Country Music band from Sweden, Rivers, released a single called "Sober." Watch the video on YouTube. The lyrics support this book:

> *I don't have to keep you sober.*
> *You're betraying honesty for me*
> *'cause you're addicted.*
> *I've been trading innocence for you.*

The singer knows she's desperately attracted to this addict, but she also knows,

> *I'm the one who holds the gun.*
> *I won't pull the trigger 'til I figure out*
> *If you really don't care about it.*
> *Can you live without it?*

Ladies, it's NOT your job to get your guy to go to rehab, to get his GED, or to want to make something of his life. Trying to mother a guy not only won't work, but he'll also resent you for trying to control him!

Before you develop ulcers over a guy who's trouble, look yourself in the mirror and admit, "I accept my role in this relationship." If you're grieving over some dude's behavior, all you must do is remove one person--yourself--from the dysfunctional dance.

Sure, bad boys seem exciting. Rivers admits, "You light the [my] fire." But naïve girls stupidly mistake their heart pumping thrills for what they call "love."

This is when being solo and having quiet time is crucial. When you're completely grounded, you'll conclude your bad boy is bad for you!

<u>Gilda-Gram®</u>
If a guy's doing something *to* you
rather than *for* you, pack him in.

As I had said, girls who like bad boys don't think highly enough about themselves to believe they could snag a cool guy. But they also probably haven't seen positive relationship role models that are respectful and caring.

These girls know something is not right and they're miserable enough to ask for help. But they must also help themselves.

Is the new guy you've just met *worthy* of your emotions? To even consider that question, you must have high self-confidence, a strong inner self, and boundaries you stick to.

Too many girls tell me, "I know I have low self-esteem." If that's the case, RAISE IT! They confess, "I don't think I'm worth anything without a guy." If that's the case, CHANGE THAT.

Are you attracted to a bad boy? Take this "Bad Boy Screener" and discover the truth!

Bad Boy Screener

Answer Yes or No to each of the following questions:

___1. Are you attracted to guys who ignore you?

___2. Do you hang out with guys you don't respect?

___3. Do the guys you like hit on your girlfriends?

___4. Do you know he's bad, but think he'll change?

___5. Do the guys you like call you names, criticize your body, and diss you?

___6. Do the guys you like rarely call?

___7. Do the guys you like lie to you, flirt with girls in front of you, or cheat?

___8. Do the guys you like get into trouble at school or with the law?

___9. Do the guys you like have secret lives?

___10. Do the guys you like have bad relations with their parents?

___11. Do the guys you like still like their ex?

___12. Do the guys you like throw temper tantrums?

ScoreCard

Surprise! If you had even one Yes, you're a bad boy magnet. If you want a happy relationship, change your tastes, and act on these words:

<u>Gilda-Gram®</u>
I deserve a cool guy.

Females are notorious for wanting to change their boyfriends, even the ones who are not bad boys. They think, "My guy would be so cool--if only he'd change his taste in music; if only he'd change his baggy jeans; if only he'd change his movie tastes. It's as though their guys are not good enough when they meet them, so the girls want to give them a makeover.

No male changes because someone wants him to. And most guys resent a girl trying to make them over.

Remember the guy-pleasing girls we discussed earlier who make themselves over according to their guys' demands? An It Girl wouldn't put up with that any more than a cool guy would.

So, lay off him. If he's treating you *with disrespect*, that's your cue to leave. But before you do, here's how to give it one last try.

Quick Steps Before You Exit

1. Confront your guy in a calm way. Follow the 3-Step "When-you..., I feel..., Stop" Technique.

2. Know in advance what your boundaries are. What will you accept? What won't you tolerate? For example, know if he hits you, you're out without turning back. Also know you won't watch his tantrums.

3.   Tell him if he doesn't act nicer to you, you're not sticking around. Bullying boys back down when their girlfriends no longer become their victim.

4.   Tell him exactly what you need so he won't say later he didn't know. But be sure that once you give him the ultimatum of walking you *keep your promise.* Otherwise, your words won't count for anything, and your guy will continue his badness.

Once you've tried everything, your bad boy may still choose to remain as he is. Then either accept him or leave. If you accept your boyfriend as is you give up the right to try to change him and spending hours complaining to your friends. Your friends will tire of hearing your complaints without you taking action.

If you decide to stay, you have chosen to settle. Any girl who willingly accepts "Less-Than" treatment is unwittingly teaching her guy it's okay to treat her that way. If you're still with him after bad treatment, you've willingly bought into his antics.

If you decide to leave, you'll especially need solo time to figure out what you saw in him. After completely recovering from your breakup, you should feel apathetic to anything he does now. That's when you're ready to love someone new and nicer.

How to Recognize Cool Guys

What do cool guys look like? How do they act? How do they treat a girl? Drew Barrymore said, "A great boyfriend doesn't pee on your parade . . . He'll get out of the car and pick you a few flowers." Brandy says, "It's the little things that count--like a phone call when you least expect it." Yes, cool guys have your back!

Cool Guy Selector

The traits cool guys demonstrate are:

1. Attentiveness

3. Affection

4. Devotion

5. Compassion

6. Dependability

7. Generosity

8. Loyalty

9. Trust

10. Honesty

11. Stability

12. Fidelity

In addition to these basics, cool guys will want to care for you when you're sick, compliment you when you look especially good or do something well, enjoy your friends and family, be happy when something makes you happy, remember special occasions, enjoy spending quiet time together, and give you your space to be solo. They also use the pronouns "we," "us," and "ours."

Sometimes cool guys are so cool, girls take them for granted. That's a big mistake because if you date a cool guy, a wiser girl will. No girl has time to seek cool guy traits if she's hanging with losers.

Being Self-Sufficient

The great thing about being with a cool guy is that he appreciates the different aspects of your life and he wants to help you enjoy them. He's a part of your heart, but he's not the sole reason you get up in the morning. One of the qualities a cool guy finds attractive in you is your ability to be self-sufficient.

During a TV show, I met a good looking high ranking military officer. He had just gotten married and he wanted to share with me a photo of his new bride. When I saw she was in a wheelchair, I asked about that. He explained she's permanently disabled, but "Of all the women I know, she's the only one who *wanted* me, rather than *needed* me!" He beamed, "She's the most self-sufficient lady I know." Despite this woman's lifetime disability, she loves herself—and that's what her new husband fell in love with.

How to Adore the Person You Are

Who are you? Don't describe your outside packaging, like your blonde hair, green eyes, long legs, zits, frizzy hair, or 10 extra pounds. We're not talking about the external traits that often make girls feel

194

inadequate for not competing with airbrushed or computer-generated images in magazines.

Who you are consists of your inner traits, like your devotion to animals, your humor, or your kindness toward the elderly. These are just a few qualities of inner self that describe you.

Describe more here:

_____

This is a difficult exercise because we're used to thinking of ourselves in terms of externals. Here are some responses from girls with strong inner selves:

"I have a strong will and I won't allow myself to be misled."

"I know my power and I don't let anyone try to take it from me."

"I am nurturing, but before I nurture other people I nurture myself."

Here are some other responses from girls who need to develop inner self muscle:

"I am shy and quiet so people tend to take advantage of me."

"I'm a pushover for people when they pressure me."

"When I'm with friends, I keep my opinions to myself even when I know I'm right."

If your responses don't express the *real* you, take another look. Understand you are beautiful from the inside out. Know that, appreciate that, honor that.

Once you're feeling independent and self-sufficient, you'll know you don't *need* a boyfriend. Although you might *want* a boyfriend, you'll understand that the most important thing in your life is to believe in YOU!

NEED #4

Accept Only "Got-Your-Back" Love

Dear Dr. Gilda,

There is this guy in my class and we've been friends forever. Last month he asked me out. After I said "no" he was heartbroken. Now we don't talk.

I've decided I like him after all, and I want to go out with him but I don't know if he still likes me. I am too shy to ask him out. What if he says "no"? I can't take the risk. Please help me!!
Kate

<u>Gilda-Gram®</u>
Friendship with a guy
is the first step to love.

Dear Kate,

This guy knows that something's up between you, or he would never have taken that bold step to ask you out. You surprised him by saying "no." So he backed off.

Now you say you've changed your mind. Since you're not sure whether he still likes you and he refuses to endure another humiliation, you've got to swallow your pride and level with him. Tell him the truth that his invitation caught you by surprise, and now you'd like to reconsider.

If he's into playing games, he may try to give you back some of your own medicine. But if he's really a cool guy he'll be delighted. It's certainly worth a shot because if you don't try, he'll never know you'd like to reconsider.
Dr. Gilda

I receive many emails from women of all ages from all over the world who want to advance their relationship with their guy friends. Each fears ruining a terrific friendship if the romance tanks.

Dear Dr. Gilda,
How do I tell a guy I love him when he's my best friend?
May

Dear Dr. Gilda,
All the guys I ever liked are my really good friends. How do I make them realize I can be more?
Ellie

Dear Dr. Gilda,
I'm in love with my best friend. We just recently became great friends, but I trust him with my life and I tell him everything. Sometimes, it seems like we're a couple. But I don't know if he feels the same.

I'm afraid if I say anything, our friendship would become weird. I don't want to lose his friendship, but I

have deep feelings for him. What do I do?
Star

Dear Dr. Gilda,

I've fallen in love with my best guy friend. He doesn't know how I feel. Should I tell him or keep it to myself? This situation happened to me once before, and it turned out horribly. I was really into one of my guy friends, he found out, and he told me he didn't like me as a girlfriend. Now we don't talk.

I'm afraid of this happening again! What should I do? I don't want to ruin our friendship. Dazed and Confused in LA

I recently met a couple in their 40s who had just gotten married. They had been best friends for 20 years, went on trips around the world together, confided in each other every day, but never had a romance. After two decades, their friends began to ask, "The way you two look at each other makes us all think something deep is going on." The pair had never considered this possibility. But they considered it now. Today they're a successful and respectful pair whose love just exudes when they communicate!

Sometimes this kind of connection won't work. A girl may write to me about some guy she's not attracted to as a boyfriend, yet he's a fab friend.

But girls interested in going beyond friendship status worry that if they confess their feelings and the guy rejects them, tears may flow. Besides the rejection potential, nobody wants to lose a good pal.

We can't predict a guy's response. So how can a girl get promoted from friend to girlfriend?

Clues That Suggest A Possible Future

1. He keeps his word about calling.

2. He gives you details about his life and doesn't mention other girls.

3. He suggests doing different activities with you each week.

4. He cracks up at your jokes.

5. His looks into your eyes become longer and more intense.

6. His hand on your hand or shoulder lingers longer than usual.

7. He programmed your number as a favorite on his phone.

8. Friends say he talks respectfully about you when you're not around.

9. He waits for you after school.

10. He gave you a special gift for your birthday.

11. He notices your new clothes.

12. He doesn't introduce you as his "friend," but uses your name.

13. He talks to you on the phone for a long time.

14. He'd rather hang with you than anyone else.

Of course, these signs could mean you and your guy are just great friends and he could simply be acting *very* friendly. Or as much as he's trying to hide it, he may actually be thinking "she's lots of fun" and is moving toward "she's the one." What should you do next?

Don't suggest outright that the two of you date. Remember, he's the hunter and hunters like to do the hunting without a girl's bold help.

Use your humor to continue to enjoy each other. If anything more is to happen it will. What's really the rush?

Let your shoulder touch his while you're discussing homework. Look deep into his eyes. Smile. Support your leaning shoulder with smiling words. A smiling attitude is a super-powered guy magnet. If your body language and voice are encouraging his, you'll observe certain Signs of Encouragement.

Signs of Encouragement

1. You're out as "friends" but he insists on paying.

2. His face turns red when he's near you.

3. His body language moves in sync with yours. If your legs are crossed, so are his. If one of your hands is in your pocket, so is his. If he reflects your body language, it suggests you're in sync.

Don't blow it by taking the reins away from him

and scaring him off. He's as uncomfortable about being rejected as you are.

Gilda-Gram®
**It Girls charm a guy,
not alarm a guy.**

Occasionally, a guy just won't get it. That's when it might be good to resort to using words. Again, you don't want to feel foolish so instead of suggesting the two of you become an item, try this test: "David (Always use his name for closeness and seriousness.), could you imagine if we were a couple?" Let his mind process the thought.

If he dismisses the idea quickly, he may not be interested—or he's too scared to admit it. If he laughs it off, there may be some hope. If he says, "we'd never make it together. You're too demanding and so am I," you know he might have thought about it, but has decided it won't work.

Once a guy is set against a relationship, even if you stripped naked and professed undying love, his "no" means "no"—at least for now. (On second thought, if you did strip naked for him, he would probably agree to have sex with you--but walk out later, anyway. Who needs that?) Someday, he might change his mind. But for now, dude's off limits and it's best to keep the relationship a friendship.

Let's suggest another possibility. You're already a team, but you know he dates other girls. You want a committed relationship. What can you do?

To Commit or Split?

He thinks "fling," but you think "real thing." So you both envision different relationships! Can you move him along?

You probably won't like this answer, but the word is "patience." Of course, if you already know your stud is an out-and-out bad boy who wants a bevy of girls, there's nothing that will change him from player to stayer.

But what if you and your guy are beginning to get close? You see it, feel it, and know it, but he's never broached the topic.

Gilda-Gram®
Patience is golden.

Dear Dr. Gilda,
Brian is so cool. We go to different schools but I think he likes me. How long should I wait until I ask him out?
Mimi

Dear Mimi,
If you're an It Girl, you're immersed in the activities you love. You won't wait around for this dude to make a move. You sense he likes you but you're so busy, you often forget him.

Talk to him about the interests you share, and perhaps make plans to do some together. Observe his behaviors as a friend and note whether you even want him as a boyfriend.

If he's interested in you for romance, you'll eventually know.
Dr. Gilda

Although you're giving your guy cues you're interested in growing your friendship, remember to let the hunter hunt. If he takes a long time to make a move, accept that YOUR timetable is not necessarily his.

Gilda-Gram®
**Guys operate on guy time.
Nothing girls do will quicken their pace.**

Pushing a guy to act more quickly could backfire if he feels controlled and manipulated. Focus on the things you've got going for YOU--whether Dude comes around or not. When girls aren't patient, they get hurt.

Dear Dr. Gilda,
I'm 25, and I really want a long relationship with someone. I've been in love before, but things didn't work out. That was two years ago. I can't find someone with whom I can have a solid relationship. Every guy seems not to want commitment.
Sara

Dear Sara,
Isn't it amazing that you keep finding commitment-phobic guys when you *say* you want the opposite? It Girls who want to settle down find guys with the same goals. Since we attract people like ourselves, ask yourself whether you're absolutely certain

you want a committed guy.

Also, you want love so much you probably come on too strong. Examine your behavior and determine whether you're projecting cues that are repelling, rather than attracting, cool guys.
Dr. Gilda

Sure enough, Sara returned with a list of telltale qualities in three of the guys she had dated. She admitted that because she was so intent on permanently hooking up, she missed their Don't-Go-There cues:

1. a guy who had just broken off a two-year relationship

2. a guy who was moving to another country

3. a guy who would only marry into his own faith, which Sara was not part of.

From the list, Sara could see that although the guys were generous and kind, they were definitely not commitment-ready. She vowed on her next dates to ask more questions before wanting to get close. Good for Sara!

Manipulating too much too soon lands many girls in trouble. I often receive emails after the damage is done, when it's too late for my advice.

Dear Dr. Gilda,
There's a guy I've liked for a year and a half. For a couple of months, we've been messing around seriously. The problem is he doesn't want to commit. I cry a lot when I think we might part. I enjoy being with

him, but I don't want to ask for a commitment because I don't want to scare him off.

I've never loved anyone as much as I love him. Everything about him is perfect. Please help.
Susan

Dear Susan,

You're miserable, yet you call this relationship "perfect"? You're already "messing around" with him, and from the tone of your letter I assume he's seeing other girls. In most cases, messing around means you're intimate.

Guys want to know WIIFM? ("What's In It For Me?") to make a commitment to you. Most guys will "mess around" with a mule if it were available. So the fact that *you* love *him* probably means very little to the future of your duo.

After a year and a half, you've gotten to see what your guy wants to do about your association. Nothing! Refrain from intimacy and see if that's the only thing holding him to you.

Sure, you might be hurt if he leaves, but having spent this much time together already, you don't want it to go on any longer if he's not planning to come around. If your honesty scares him away, he's an insensitive user, and it's best you find out now. But if he has your back and doesn't want to lose you, he'll make a move toward permanence.
Dr. Gilda

In committed relationships, when two people are

giving as much as they are receiving, there is less chance they will be disappointed and hurt. Remember the lesson from *The Little Prince?* The Little Prince *invested* in the flower, and therefore felt closer to her. When two people invest time and emotions in each other, neither wants to lose the investment they've built over time.

Young women must wait for their guys to feel "invested." But waiting would not seem as an eternity if girls eliminated the guy as their central focus and enjoyed their life. Sara seems too desperate for love. Susan agreed to "mess around" before her guy was invested. Now what's his pay-off to continue?

It Girls think twice before they decide to put out. Sure, it's a strategy which some folks call game playing. But it's not a game for a girl to enjoy her life and say she's not available when she really isn't!

Gilda-Gram®
**Trying to hurry love
only hurries heartache.**

Dear Dr. Gilda,
A group of guys in my school started a rock band. They did a concert last week and one of the guys, Jason, was singing directly to me. I sent him a love note with my name and address. He still hasn't called. Then I sent him a pair of my panties with my signature. I haven't heard from him. What now?
Denise

Dear Denise,

You've been aggressive about how you feel towards Jason and he never responded. Translation: he's not interested.

A performer's job is to flirt with his audience. You bought the act. Realize it was only an act. I bet you weren't the only girl who slipped him her digits (although I'm not sure about the panties).

There's a difference between letting a guy know you're available and being a pest. You don't want Jason to laugh you off as a love-starved chick. Lick your wounds, accept the gig for what it was, and find someone emotionally available.
Dr. Gilda

Guys need more time than girls to recognize what they're feeling. There's no point in rushing a romance that can't be rushed.

Tips for Cooling Your Jets

1. Give him time to discover how valuable you are to him. Let him reach this conclusion on his own.

2. Stop trying to rush him down the aisle before he's out of diapers. He'll only run faster.

3. Don't become overly emotional. A girl's deep emotions often frighten guys who've been trained to avoid vulnerability.

4. Don't try to trick a guy to commit by making him jealous, getting pregnant, moving in with him, or doing only what he wants while ignoring your needs. He'll dislike these tricks to snag him.

5. There are few guys who won't commit. But it will always be according to their timeline.

When you take your time, you'll make your guy your teammate, instead of unsuccessfully trying to manipulate him into becoming your soulmate.

<u>Gilda-Gram®</u>
A teammate watches your back,
because you're on the same team.
A soulmate watches your back,
because he loves you.

Soulmates become Teammates first. Teammates share your goals, dreams, and values. They feel comfortable knowing there's no love pressure. They see you as a friend they can trust. They show you their feelings, the same feelings they'd ordinarily hide from a girl they like. They'll watch out for you.

As you enjoy a teammate for whom he is, he won't act like an insecure dork trying to impress you. He'll trust you and you'll get to know him well. This friendship is crucial before real love can set in.

<u>Gilda-Gram®</u>
Friends first,
lovers later.

Since you're an It Girl, you've got the power to choose whether this teammate even *deserves* to become your soulmate. You have all the time you want to observe his behavior and decide.

CONCLUSION
You're In Charge!

As you now know, to attract cool guys your focus must be on *you,* not on a guy. You know this attitude works because it's usually the guys you have no interest in who are interested in you!!

Match.com published an article I wrote for them called, "Does Your Honey Have Your Back?" In it, I said, "People who love each other take action when their partner needs protection."

The article said, "When Sandra Bullock won a Golden Globe in 2010 for *The Blind Side,* her acceptance speech was, 'To my husband: There's no surprise that my work got better when I met you, because I never knew what it felt like for someone to have my back.'

Women audibly sighed over that romantic testimonial, as they wondered whether *their* guys had *their* backs. (I was one of those women.) At the time, I was dating someone who was crazy about me—but obviously not crazy *enough,* since we are no longer together. Prompted by Bullock's speech, I had asked him, "Do you have my back?" His shocking response was, 'You're such a strong woman. Why would you need anyone to have your back?' Wrong answer, Boyfriend; everyone wants to feel protected by the person he or she loves—as strong or as weak as that person might appear. *Sayonara!*"

Sadly, not long after her acceptance speech, the world watched Sandra Bullock's marriage collapse when her husband was caught cheating. From this we learn that a guy's mere *saying* he has your back is not the same as his *showing* he does.

<u>Gilda-Gram®</u>
Back protection signals love intention.

Sure, we all want to think we're capable and self-sufficient when we're on our own. But the world often gets messy. So having an extra pair of eyes, ears, and hands to guide us can prove love in action.

Having someone's back trumpets the strength of commitment between two people. But back protection must be mutual. Don't expect a guy to care about you, if you're not willing to demonstrate caring for him, too. According to Psychology Today, some signs of a healthy relationship are: partners supporting each other, sharing their emotions, and expressing their gratitude.

Tony was living with Jana. She had a terrible sinus infection, and was advised to inhale steam to help her breathe. When she went into the bedroom to make their bed, without being asked, Tony boiled a pot of water, and added special herbs, to heal his honey's condition. When Jana returned to the kitchen, as sick as she felt, she was surprised, and very appreciative.

Maria was dating George, a medical school student. As a diabetic, she told him she discovered that when she ate seaweed, her blood sugar numbers dropped. As weird as George thought this was, he went out of his way to research this possibility at his medical school. Sure enough, he found published studies showing positive outcomes for diabetics who use oral medication and also eat seaweed. Maria was very touched that George a) took her findings seriously, b) inconvenienced himself to question his own traditional medical training, and c) cared so obviously about Maria's well-being.

At 28, Janice was already a famous author. She was also mother of two young children, and wife for 10 years of a prominent stockbroker. Janice wore a prosthetic leg and severely limped due to an auto accident she was in when she was just 16. Despite his own very prosperous career, her handsome and devoted husband put aside his work to read every article and book she would write.

These are just a few examples of how each guy had his lady's back. What better way is there to prove true love?

Your job is to ignore the ego-boosting words a guy throws your way, and instead pay attention to how he goes *out of his way* for you.

Dear Dr. Gilda,

For the past 4 years, I have liked the same guy. But every time I got close to him, he'd push me away. Now I'm in college, and I've met a guy in a band I like. Since the guy I liked all these years found out about my new crush, he's acting jealous. Why is he now finally giving me what I always wanted?
Crushing Real Bad

Dear Crushing,
You are in good company! After Ben Affleck humiliated his then-wife Jennifer Garner by allegedly cheating on her with their nanny, a gossip magazine said he was "absolutely fuming" when she started dating again. While he didn't value her enough to be faithful, as soon as she re-started her love life with someone else, he had plenty to say.

Similarly, when you put all your attention on the guy you liked, he ran away. But when you became interested in someone else, this guy realized what he had lost. In general, when a girl is too easily available, many guys sadly tend to take her for granted—until she reminds herself she's an It Girl—and walks away!
Dr. Gilda

Gilda-Gram®
**Be self-involved,
not male-involved.**

This healthy approach to love is not based on game playing. It's based on *loving* yourself and *being* yourself.

But please understand this: I don't mean you

should become so egocentric that you discount everyone else's needs. What I'm saying is that you must take care of your needs by honoring them and enjoying them first, while also being open to others.

When you demonstrate you're into your own exciting life, a guy becomes interested in how he can grab your attention and fit into it alongside you.

Gilda-Gram®
Don't let your HE meter
dictate your ME meter.

Now you're an It Girl, or at least on your way to becoming one! A guy who wins an It Girl's heart is consistent in his behavior, calls when he says he will, and keeps his word. He knows that she knows she has choices, and if he doesn't behave like a cool and respectful guy, it will be "goodbye."

Gilda-Gram®
It Girls ditch fickle guys who adore them today,
but ignore them tomorrow.

But when It Girls start being It Girls, they sometimes question whether they have the right to demand a guy's compassion. Vicki was such a girl.

Dear Dr. Gilda,
   I am 25, and I have been dating an attractive dentist for a few weeks. After a night's passionate sleepover, both of us rushed to get to work. It had snowed heavily during the night. He cleaned off his car, got into it, and waved goodbye, leaving me stranded to

struggle to get the snow off my car. I felt dissed that he didn't spend a few minutes helping me. Am I wrong?
Vicki

Dear Vicki,
You're not wrong to want a man who's considerate, especially after you shared your body during an intimate night. Clearly, Dr. Dentist didn't have your back. Are you sure you want to spend any more time with a man who doesn't?
Dr. Gilda

Answers to the questions women ask me are not always obvious. Many females defend all the reasons they like a guy, but put off dealing with the one vital point of this book: "Don't Lie on Your Back for a Guy Who Doesn't Have Yours"!!! Then they seek me out after their heart has been broken. All their tears can be prevented if they take care of themselves from the start.

Dear Dr. Gilda,
I'm a 19-year-old sophomore in college. I love to travel and I have been to Europe four times. Next semester, I will be in Russia and after that I'll study in Tahiti. I have an idea of what I want to do in my life. When I am at school I want to travel, but when I come home it will be different. I still want to do a lot, but I also think about my future of being with a special guy and having kids.

My mom wants me to have kids now! She wants me to do what I want, but I think she'd prefer that I "settle down."

During the summer, I met a guy from Portugal

who was visiting his relatives here. He decided to move to the United States. Since I am on school break, we have been seeing each other and it seems perfect. I don't want to "Bet on the Prince!," as the title of one of your books is called, but I don't think any girl with a guy like this could ask for more.

He is everything I would want for my future. He is family-oriented, he wants kids the same time I do (at about 27 years old), he is good looking and has a good body, he likes everything about me, he compliments me, he pays for everything, he likes to work, he respects my needs and wants, and the list goes on.

So, what's the problem? He says he wants to be with me but I am leaving and he said he's not going to "wait." He says he doesn't want a girlfriend, but if I were here he would. He doesn't go out of his way to meet women, but if he does meet someone else, what will happen to us?

At this age, I feel I shouldn't be thinking about things like this, but you can see why I would want to keep him. I don't know if I should tell him how I feel. I think sometimes he is sad that I am always leaving to go somewhere. He knows I have a lot of goals, but those would come after I finish school.

I don't know what to do. Thank you.
Meredith

Dear Meredith,
Your life seems wonderfully fulfilling. But now you're torn between what your mom is pressuring you to do and what your heart is saying. Since you're

amazingly excited about your life, it would be pitiful for you to give that up for a future with someone you know so little.

When someone walks away from a fabulous career or opportunity to be in a couple, during the pair's first argument, pent up resentment can emerge. "Look what I gave up for you!" could become part of your angry rhetoric.

Whatever you do, this is not the time for you to settle down and have babies, as your mom would like. At least, you and your guy have already decided that's not in your immediate future. He may be everything you THINK you want right now, but at the beginning, every love affair appears perfect. Time will prove whether it really is. You are certainly not prepared to give up what you have already achieved, or to continue life without your college degree.

For the time being, enjoy every moment for what it is. Definitely share your concerns with him. Encourage him to similarly open his heart to you. When two people love each other, they protect their partners' backs by supporting each other's dreams.

Your time together doesn't have to be immediate! Think of the wonderful trips you can take as you visit each other, while you're independently building your resumes!
Dr. Gilda

Meredith is an It Girl. She is focused on the things she loves and is intent to fulfill her goals. Her mom and her new guy are pressuring her to abandon her dreams in favor of theirs. That's not "Got-Your-Back" Love on either of their parts.

A guy should *enhance* the life a girl already has, not try to prevent her from achieving it. If this guy is meant to be with Meredith in the years to come, he'll be there.

Gilda-Gram®
If he's yours, you can't lose him.
If he's not, you don't need him.

It Girl principles reflect a girl's inner strength. When a girl is strong inside, she attracts strong, sensational guys. And they want to offer her their protection because they care. Then the girl's biggest problem becomes which guy to choose from all the cool ones pursuing her!

***

Benefit from
Dr. Gilda's personal Advice & Coaching
www.DrGilda.com

***

MORE BOOKS BY DR. GILDA

Dr. Gilda's Self-Worth Series
-- "I'm Worth Loving! Here's Why."
-- "Ask for What You Want—AND GET IT!
-- "How to Be a Worry-Free Woman"

Dr. Gilda's Relationship Series
--8 Steps to a Sizzling Marriage
--8 Tips to Understand the Opposite Sex
--10 Questions Single Women Should Never Ask
    & 10 They Should
--10 Signs of a Cheater-to-Be

Dr. Gilda's Fidelity Series
--Why Your Cheater Keeps Cheating—And You're
    Still There!
--How to Cope with the Cheater You Love—and WIN
--99 Prescriptions for Fidelity: *Your Rx for Trust*

ALSO
--Don't Bet on the Prince! *How to Have the Man You
Want by Betting on Yourself*
--Don't Lie on Your Back for a Guy Who Doesn't
Have Yours

***

Dr. Gilda Carle (Ph.D.) is an internationally known media personality and relationship expert. She has authored 15 books, including "Don't Bet on the Prince!" (a test question on "Jeopardy!"), "Teen Talk with Dr. Gilda," "He's Not All That!," "How to WIN When Your Mate Cheats" (winner of The London Book Festival literary award), "99 Prescriptions for Fidelity," and more. She also wrote the weekly "30-Second Therapist" column for the Today Show, and the "Ask Dr. Gilda" advice columnist for Match.com.

On TV, Dr. Gilda was the regular therapist for

the Sally Jessy Raphael show, the "Love Doc" for MTV Online, and the TV host of "The Dr. Gilda Show" pilot for Twentieth Century Fox. In addition, she was the therapist in HBO's Emmy Award winner, "Telling Nicholas," featured on Oprah, where she guided a family to tell their 7-year-old that his mom died in the World Trade Center bombing.

In academia and the corporate sector, she is a product spokesperson, Professor Emerita, motivational speaker, and management consultant.

Through her website, www.DrGilda.com, Dr. Gilda provides Advice and Coaching throughout the world.

As President of Country Cures, Inc., a non-profit 501(c)(3) educational charity, she is the "Country Music Doctor." She uniquely uses Country Music to provide Civilian Success Skills for Homeless Female Veterans and their children. If you or someone you know can benefit from this help, please visit www.CountryCures.org.

Reach Dr. Gilda at
www.DrGilda.com
or
www.CountryCures.org

Made in the USA
San Bernardino, CA
18 March 2017